SNOW SENSE

A GUIDE TO EVALUATING SNOW AVALANCHE HAZARD

By:

Jill Fredston and Doug Fesler

Edited by:

Karl Birkeland and Doug Chabot

Alaska Mountain Safety Center, Inc.
Anchorage, Alaska

Produced/Distributed by:
Alaska Mountain Safety Center, Inc. (AMSC)
9140 Brewster's Drive
Anchorage, AK 99516-6928
Phone/Fax: (907) 345-3566
(snowsensebook@gmail.com or alaskamountain@gmail.com)

Book design: Marie McConkey and Carolina Rodriguez, Designers
                John Ray, Production Coordinator

All photographs by the authors or editors unless otherwise indicated.

Cover photograph by Jim Bay (mtnlight@telus.net), Columbia
Mountains, Revelstoke, B.C., Canada.

NOTE: All conversions between English and Metric units in this
book are approximations only.

Snow Sense: a guide to evaluating snow avalanche hazard / by Jill
Fredston and Doug Fesler—5th edition.

ISBN: 978-0-615-49935-2

Printed in Alaska

PRINTED ON
RECYCLED PAPER

Table of Contents

Preface

This book is intended for anyone who travels, works, or plays in avalanche country anywhere in the world. Our goal is to help backcountry travelers learn to recognize, evaluate, and avoid potential snow avalanche hazards.

A *snow avalanche* is a mass of snow moving downhill that may also contain ice, soil, rocks, or other debris. Because most avalanche accidents involving recreationists result from human-triggered slab releases, the focus of *Snow Sense* is on slab avalanches.

Avalanches do not happen by accident; they occur only at certain times, in certain places, and for particular reasons. We strongly believe that the majority of avalanche accidents can be avoided by learning to integrate and heed vital pieces of information. *Snow Sense* provides a framework for evaluating avalanche hazard. It is not a substitute for field experience. If you want to learn about dragons, you need to go to the den of the dragon—but sometimes a dragon book helps.

If you treat avalanches like games of chance, the odds are against you. (Photo by Janet Kellam)

Introduction

If I could ever see my son again, I would hug him once, hug him again, and then punch him in the gut. He knew better than this.

I didn't feel comfortable snowboarding on that slope. But no one else said anything. If I had spoken my mind, maybe my friends would still be alive.

I wanted to help him get his snowmobile unstuck. When I rode above him and turned, the snow gave way beneath me. The last time I saw my brother, he was tumbling like a ragdoll...

We'd been making loops around the bowl for about an hour, just having a ball. My partners weren't even riding. They were just sitting on the flats below us, hanging out in the sunshine.

These quotes should give you an idea of what your friends and relatives will say if you die in an avalanche. Each of us, every day, is an accident trying not to happen. If we didn't take risks, we might forget we are alive. But if we assume risks blindly, we are likely to pay a high price in consequences.

Year after year, avalanches claim victims around the world in stunningly similar accidents. Only the names seem to change. Of the avalanches catching backcountry enthusiasts, roughly 95% are triggered by the victims or their partners. Contrary to myth, it is not noise or random bad luck that causes the problem, but the weight and impact of those on or near the slope.

While some accidents are a result of not recognizing potential hazard, most occur because the victims either underestimate the hazard or overestimate their ability to deal with it, typically exercising poor route selection, travel procedures, or choice of timing. Many of the accidents involve "experienced" mountain travelers rather than rank beginners. The assumption that those who excel at their sport are equally skilled at evaluating avalanche hazard and making objective decisions has repeatedly proven deadly.

Every accident, of any kind, is preceded by a chain of events or a series of errors, but each is set into motion at one irreversible moment. Until that moment, the accident might have been prevented. Usually, avalanche accident investigations reveal that victims overlooked or ignored not just one or two clues, but three or more by the time their group ran into trouble. Few people choose to cross a busy four-lane highway without listening for the traffic or looking both ways. Similarly, travelling on or near steep, snow-covered slopes without gathering and integrating information about the current stability of the snow is like wearing earplugs and blinders. Besides learning to read "nature's billboards," the key is to not allow ourselves to get distracted by our own agendas.

Steep slopes can be negotiated safely but it is a matter of timing. Avalanches are like fish—they tend to run in schools. When avalanches are running, it is more important than ever to carefully evaluate snow stability and choose good routes every step of the way. There will be some days when only lower angle slopes can be travelled safely and steeper slopes need to be avoided. There will be other days when you can safely travel on everything in sight, no matter the angle or aspect.

Because the snowpack is stable most of the time, it is common to travel to a particular spot in avalanche terrain repeatedly without seeing any avalanches. As a result, we get "positive reinforcement," that is, we begin to think of an area as safe. But if we visit that location often enough, sooner or later we will encounter unstable conditions. To travel safely in dragon country, you need to think like a dragon. Learn where they live and feed, when they sleep, and what fires them to life.

Principal Types of Avalanches

Avalanches, which occur in both wet and dry snow, come in all shapes and sizes. Even the smallest can result in harm if you happen to be in the wrong place at the wrong time. The four main types are loose snow avalanches, slab avalanches, cornice collapses, and ice avalanches. Of these, slab avalanches catch the greatest number of backcountry travelers because they release on terrain frequented by recreationists and involve snow that fractures catastrophically across a relatively large area.

LOOSE SNOW AVALANCHES

Loose snow avalanches, also called sluffs and point releases, start with a small amount of *cohesionless* snow and typically pick up more snow as they descend. From a distance, they appear to start at a point and fan out into a triangle. They are usually small, involving only upper layers of snow, but they are capable of being quite large and destructive depending upon how much material they

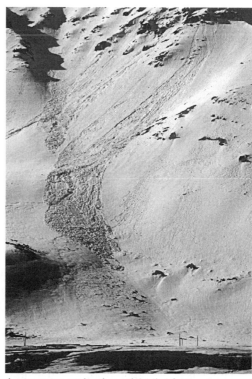

Loose snow avalanches originating from sun-warmed snow near rocks.

entrain. To ice climbers and other backcountry travelers, loose snow avalanches are particularly hazardous when the consequences of being swept off a stance onto rough terrain are serious. The stress of the moving snow in a loose snow slide can also trigger larger, deeper slab releases.

Dry loose snow releases occur most often on steep slopes (generally 40°+), during or shortly after low density snowfall, or after a period of cold, clear weather has reduced the cohesion of the surface snow. Wet loose snow avalanches release during warming events caused by rain, rising temperatures, or solar radiation.

SLAB AVALANCHES

Slab avalanches occur when one or more layers of *cohesive* snow release as a unit. As the slab moves downhill, it begins breaking up into smaller and smaller blocks or clods. The upper boundary of the slab is the *fracture line or crown face,* while the area immediately above this is known as the *crown*. The sides of the slab are called the *flanks* and the bottom boundary is the *stauchwall*. The *bed surface* is the main sliding surface under the slab.

Remembering these terms is much less important than understanding that an avalanche may be triggered either from within or even long distances outside of any of these boundaries. The bed surface is particularly critical because it has a surface area roughly 100 times greater than the combined surface area of all the other slab boundaries. In a slab release, typically the first failure to occur is the bond between the slab and the bed surface. This places tremendous stress on the other boundary regions that, in turn, are unable to hold the slab in place.

Slab thickness can range from less than an inch to 30 feet (10 m) or more. Human-triggered slabs are generally less than 5 feet (1.5 m)

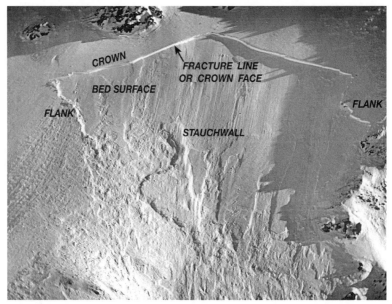

(Photo from Chuck O'Leary collection, AMSC)

deep, with many less than 2 feet (.6 m). **How deep a slab has to be to be dangerous depends entirely upon the consequences of getting caught.** Slab avalanches only a few inches thick have killed recreationists. Often, slabs are triggered where they are thinnest and the fracture then propagates into deeper snow. The depth of any given fracture line can be quite variable depending upon snow distribution across the slope. Similarly, slab avalanches can be just a few yards wide or the fracture line can extend more than a mile. The width of a "typical" human-triggered avalanche is less than 200 feet (60 m).

Slab material is also highly variable. Slabs may be hard or soft, wet or dry. The most delightful powder snow you will ever encounter may be capable of fracturing as a slab if it is relatively cohesive compared to the underlying snow.

The velocity of moving slabs is determined by the density of the snow involved as well as by the configuration of the avalanche path (i.e., slope steepness, roughness, shape, and total vertical drop). Wet slabs can move at speeds of roughly 20-65 miles per hour (10-30 meters/second) while fast-moving dry slides can have speeds ranging from about 45-150 mph (20-70 m/s). Some avalanches accelerate very quickly—a victim of a dry slab avalanche can be moving a heart-pumping 30 mph (13 m/s) within two or three seconds of getting caught.

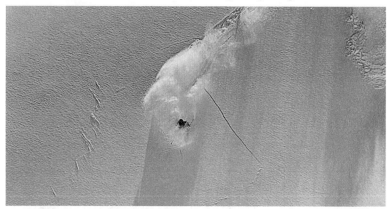

As you can see from the cracks propagating around the skier in the first photograph, all it took to trigger this soft slab avalanche was one turn. In less than the time it will take you to read this caption, the slab was in motion. The skier managed to stay on his feet and escape uninjured. (Photos taken Shukshan Arm backcountry area, Mount Baker, North Cascades, Washington by Garrett Grove)

CORNICE COLLAPSES

Cornices form when windblown snow builds out horizontally at sharp terrain breaks such as ridgecrests and the sides of gullies. Cornices can snap off well back from their edges in response to new snow or wind-loading, warming, or the weight of a person. When cornices hit the wind-loaded, pillowed area on the slope below, it is not uncommon for them to trigger bigger releases—they can be very effective "bombs." Additionally, *cornice crevasses* are often associated with cornices. These are cracks that form between the snow that is well anchored to the ridge and that which is free-hanging and thus more easily deformed. Cornice crevasses may be covered by new or wind-deposited snow and may not be readily visible to unwary travelers.

Triggered by explosives, these large cornice blocks bounced and slid nearly 800 vertical feet (244 m). Acting much like rockfall, cornice blocks can veer off the fall line by more than 30°. The large block on the left weighs roughly 64,000 pounds (~29,000 kg). The snowpack on the slope was so stable that even blocks this size did not trigger a slab release. The small photo below shows a typical cornice while the inset depicts basic nomenclature associated with cornices.

TYPICAL BREAKOFF ZONE

WIND DIRECTION →

CORNICE

WINDWARD

RIDGE

LEEWARD

OLD SNOWPACK

SNOW PILLOW

ICE AVALANCHES

Ice avalanches are caused by the collapse of unstable ice blocks (seracs) from a steep or overhanging part of a glacier. They can entrain a considerable amount of rock, ice, and snow and can travel impressively long distances. While potential ice avalanche hazard is relatively easy to recognize, it is virtually impossible to predict exactly when the ice is going to break. Contrary to lore, ice avalanches do not occur at regular intervals or even during particular periods of the day. In regions of the world where tidewater or lake level glaciers exist, there is the additional threat of surge waves caused by the ice mass plunging into the water (referred to as calving events). If you are traveling in areas threatened by ice avalanches, be willing to accept a higher level of risk. Minimize your exposure time by traveling as quickly as possible or, better yet, choose a safer route.

This high speed ice avalanche in the Alaska Range generated a wave of displaced air and snow particles (known as powderblast) that ran all the way across the valley floor. (Photo from Chuck O'Leary collection, AMSC)

OTHER AVALANCHES

Several special types of slab avalanches deserve mention. *Glide avalanches* involve release of the entire snowpack on the ground. They initiate from *glide cracks*, which are tensile fissures that typically open at varying rates of speed (usually days or weeks) in warm, homogenous, deep snowpacks. Glide cracks are generally found in areas with smooth ground surfaces such as grass or rock slabs that are well lubricated with free water from snowmelt, rain, or groundwater. The cracks are formed as the entire snowpack slips or glides downslope. Glide avalanches may or may not occur depending on the rate and amount of deformation. Glide cracks look dangerous and the area around and below them should be avoided as it is difficult to predict if or when the snow will fracture. Often, however, the snowpack in the general vicinity is quite strong as in order for the snowpack to flow as a unit it must be well-bonded, with no major buried weak layers.

Roof avalanches, another variety of slab avalanche, have injured, buried, and killed people, crushed vehicles, and caused other serious damage. These commonly release on roofs with angles of 20°-30° or greater, but may occur on roofs of only 10°-15° given smooth sliding surfaces such as metal or plastic. Slabs usually break full-depth to the roof surface, commonly in response to additional loading, warming events, or roof-clearing operations.

Slush flows are slab releases of water-saturated snow that occur mostly in high latitude areas such as northern Norway, Canada, and Alaska where cold snowpacks are subjected to rapid, intense warming in late spring and early summer. They initiate on low slope angles, often in shallow creek beds with angles of less than 15°. Flowing much like a flash flood, they can entrain large amounts of water, mud, rocks, and vegetation. Slush flows are not to be confused with wet snow releases that commonly occur at lower latitudes in response to midwinter thaws or springtime solar radiation.

The glide cracks in the top photo developed on a well-lubricated, grassy slope during several weeks of relatively warm weather. The bottom photo shows glide avalanches releasing to the ground after failure occurred at all of the slab boundaries.

An impressive slide off a small roof. (Photo by Nan Elliot)

This slush flow in arctic Alaska was triggered in late May by a small loose snow avalanche impacting the water-saturated snow in the creek bed. The slush flow ran approximately ¾ of a mile (1.2 km), reached speeds of up to 40 mph (18 m/s), and transported very large boulders.

The Avalanche Hazard Evaluation Process

SEEKING INFORMATION

You have likely heard the fable about the four blind men in India who came upon a large elephant when traveling in the forest. Unfamiliar with such an animal, each man set about trying to examine and determine the nature of the beast. One man touched a leg and resolved that the elephant resembled a tree trunk. Another man felt the tail and had no doubt that the animal was shaped like a rope. The third man stood by the ear as it flapped back and forth and concluded that the creature was very much like a fan. The fourth man felt his way around the entire body and decided that an elephant was something enormous, almost without beginning or end.

This tale is not unlike the situation a backcountry traveler faces in attempting to evaluate potential avalanche hazard. An incomplete examination of available data leads to erroneous conclusions concerning the degree of hazard present. And the data in and of itself is not as important as the *interrelationship* of the data. Generally, no single piece of information will tell the whole story. But what information do we need?

The interaction of three variables—the terrain, snowpack, and weather—determines whether or not an avalanche is possible. Terrain is the foundation of avalanches, weather is the architect, and the snowpack is the winter's blueprint. However, to determine whether an

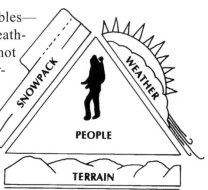

avalanche hazard exists, we must add an important fourth variable, us. Without the presence of people or property, there is no hazard.

All the information needed to evaluate potential avalanche hazard comes from these four variables and is generally available to you through observations and tests. **The bottom line is that your hazard evaluation decisions are only as good as the data you seek, integrate, and act upon.** As you travel through the mountains, choosing routes or campsites, you need to answer the following four critical questions.

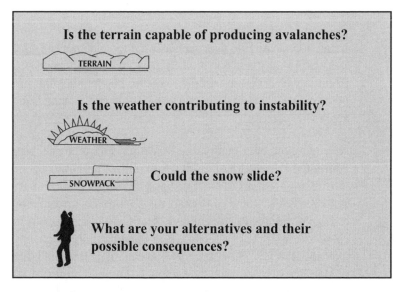

Is the terrain capable of producing avalanches?

TERRAIN

Is the weather contributing to instability?

WEATHER

SNOWPACK   Could the snow slide?

What are your alternatives and their possible consequences?

The first step is to learn to recognize avalanche terrain. Then, you can make a conscious decision about whether or not you want to expose yourself to possible hazard. If you decide that you do want to travel on or near steep slopes (and realistically, this is favored terrain of most recreationists), then you must seek the information needed to answer these questions. By doing so, you can base your hazard evaluation upon a solid foundation of facts rather than on assumptions, feelings, guesses, or fate.

❋ ❋ ❋ ❋

Is it safe or is it unsafe? The essential problem you are faced with is one of uncertainty. The key to eliminating or reducing this uncertainty lies in gathering meaningful information upon which you can build your evaluation. This process, called the *bull's-eye approach*, means getting to the heart of the problem quickly without getting bogged down or distracted by irrelevant information. The avalanche hazard evaluation process should start *before* you leave on your proposed trip, ideally with the season's first snowfall.

❋ Begin by formulating an opinion about the potential hazard based upon available data such as weather and snow advisories, topography, and personal observations. As you approach the area you'll be traveling in, look for clues indicating important recent events such as new snowfall, strong winds, and avalanche activity.

❋ As you travel, continually fine-tune your opinion by seeking additional key information that will either support or refute it. Bull's-eye data is that which has a high degree of certainty in its message. Some of the most unambiguous information available is in the form of clues reflecting the ongoing physical processes that are affecting snow stability. Stay constantly alert for all clues. Be aware that you can generally find signs of stability if you search hard enough, but indications of instability outweigh all else and should not be ignored.

❋ Be objective and keep an open mind. Don't let your desire to reach a goal interfere with your evaluation. Remember that hazard evaluation is not an event; it is a continuing process.

THE BULL'S-EYE APPROACH

Within the outer circle exists *all* of the available information, whether useful or meaningless. This marginal information does little or nothing to reduce your uncertainty about the stability of a given slope. Examples: a) the air temperature is 32°F (0°C), b) the snow depth is 3.5 feet (1.1 m), c) the slope is 800 feet high (244 m), and d) the snow is white.

Within the smaller circle exists more *relevant* data that provides you with meaningful information, but still leaves you with some uncertainty about the actual level of hazard. Examples: a) the air temperature was -4°F (-20°C) last night but is 32°F (0°C) this morning, b) 7 inches (18 cm) of new snow fell overnight, c) southeasterly winds gusting to 20 mph (10 m/s) are transporting some snow, and d) the slope is leeward with a measured angle of 36°.

Within the bull's-eye exists the most useful or *meaningful* information, with the highest degree of certainty in its message. Examples: a) there is recent avalanche activity on slopes with similar aspects and angles, b) the snow on small test slopes is fracturing when jumped on, c) stability test results indicate easy, energetic shears, and d) there are signs of significant wind-loading including hollow-sounding snow with a rippled wind slab texture and/or shooting cracks. Best yet, perhaps the slope you are concerned about avalanches while you standing safely off to the side!

DO NOT STAKE YOUR LIFE
UPON MARGINAL INFORMATION

IN SEEKING INFORMATION
GO FOR THE BULL'S-EYE!

Is The Terrain Capable of Producing an Avalanche?

The term *avalanche path* defines the area in which an avalanche may potentially occur. A large avalanche path is generally divided into three parts. The *starting or release zone* is where the unstable snow or ice breaks loose and starts to slide. The *track* is the slope or channel down which snow moves at a fairly uniform speed. The *runout or deposition zone* is where the snow slows down and comes to rest. For large avalanches, the runout zone can include a powderblast zone that extends far beyond the area of snow deposition. *Powderblast* is a wave of displaced air containing a suspension of fine-grained snow particles that often precedes the debris of fast-moving avalanches, particularly dry slabs and ice avalanches.

Complex paths may contain multiple starting zones or extensive starting zones within the track area. Sometimes small starting zones such as stream banks or small steep slopes exist in the runout zone of larger paths. In smaller paths involving little vertical drop, the starting zone and track may be indistinguishable.

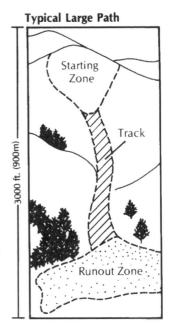

Typical Large Path

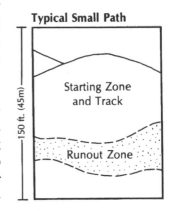

Typical Small Path

Although small, this avalanche path has all the necessary elements to be deadly. Steep and smooth, it was also leeward and loaded before it released. The debris pictured in the runout zone weighed over 2 million pounds (~907,000 kg).

Keep in mind that any steep, snow-filled slope is a potential avalanche path given the right circumstances, Even creek banks less than 40 feet (12 m) high have produced deadly avalanches.

A common mistake is to asume that avalanches occur only in large, obvious paths and to ignore the small terrain traps just beyond the parking lot. Another is to assume that it is safe to travel along the valley bottoms without considering the slopes above. The following factors influence whether a given slope is capable of producing an avalanche and will help you recognize avalanche terrain.

SLOPE ANGLE

Slope angle is the most important terrain variable determining whether or not it is possible for a given slope to avalanche. Any slope will typically have a range of slope angles but the critical determinant is the steepest portion of the slope. **The underlying concept is that as the slope angle increases, so does the stress exerted on the snowpack.**

Slab avalanches in cold snow are possible only within a certain range of slope angles, *generally* between 25° and 60°+. The word generally is highlighted because this range is variable and depends on a number of factors. Above roughly 60°, the snow tends to continually sluff off and not accumulate. Notable exceptions do occur, however, particularly in wet, maritime, or wind-affected snowpacks where very deep slab releases (>30 feet/10 meters) triggered by large cornice breaks have been observed on slopes steeper than 60°-65°. On slope angles less than approximately 25°, the friction along the bed surface is too great to allow the snow to slide. As previously described, slush flow avalanches, which occur mostly at high latitudes, commonly release on lower slope angles. (For reference, most residential staircases are around 35°.)

The greatest frequency of slab avalanches occurs on slopes with starting zone angles between 35° and 40°. Regionally, critical angles for slab failure can depend upon the snow climate, kind of avalanche, and type of weak layer. In cooler continental and intermountain climates (for example, in Colorado, where the snowpack is often thin and weak), critical or "prime time" angles *tend* to be in the mid to high 30's. In warmer, maritime climates (for example, the Pacific Northwest) with deeper and sometimes stronger snowpacks, prime time angles are typically a little steeper, ranging from the high 30's to the mid-40's. In studying numerous avalanches, it is striking how often bed surface slope angles are measured at 37° and 38°.

Your weight and motion can trigger an avalanche even if you are on a low angle slope or on the flats as long as this terrain is connected to a slope with an angle of roughly 25° and sufficient instability exists. What do we mean by connected? It

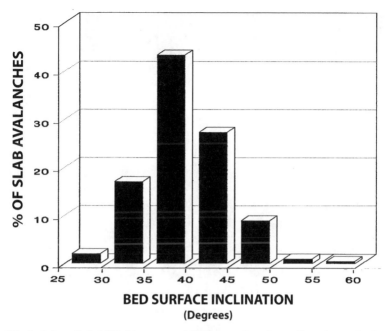

This chart shows that of 194 slabs measured, 87% occurred on slopes with angles ranging between 30° and 45°. Of these, 43% released on slope angles of 35°-40° and 27% on 40°-45° slopes. Note that only 2% of the avalanches fractured on 25°-30° slopes. Critical slope angles are dependent upon conditions and are strongly influenced by regional snow climate. (Source: Perla, 1977, Slab Avalanche Measurements, Canadian Geotechnical Journal, Volume 14, No. 2, National Research Council, Canada.)

depends upon the nature of the instability. It is very common to trigger slopes from the bottom, the edges, or the gentler angles. The more unstable the snow, the farther away from steep slopes you likely need to be. For example, under rare, extreme conditions (with impossible to miss bull's-eye clues including widespread natural avalanche activity, whumphing or collapsing noises with nearly every step, and long-running shooting cracks), we have triggered avalanches while skiing in a wide valley bottom more than a quarter of a mile (400 meters) away from the slopes that avalanched.

The survivors of this avalanche that killed two of their friends wish they had taken their helmets off and looked around. They didn't realize that the low angle gully they were riding in was connected to slopes that were so much steeper. This is a classic terrain trap.

Continually ask yourself, "Is the slope steep enough to slide?" Guessing isn't good enough—always keep an inclinometer handy so that you can *measure* slope angles. Inclinometers are small, lightweight, and inexpensive and are built into some compasses and smart phones. By putting numbers on the steepest portion of the slope, you will eliminate much of your uncertainty concerning whether or not the slope can avalanche. Measuring slope angles is also helpful for categorizing the particular kind of instability that exists on a given day. The slab depth, distribution, and structure as well as the type of weak layer will influence what slope angles are likely to avalanche. If you see recent fractures, measure the bed surface slope angles, if it is possible to do so safely, so that you can get a handle on the nature of the beast you are dealing with.

TIPS FOR MEASURING SLOPE ANGLES

Accurate slope angle measurements can be made by sighting upslope, downslope, or parallel to the slope. Caution: Avoid standing directly underneath steep slopes that have not already avalanched.

To measure slope angles accurately:

❄ Do <u>not</u> set the inclinometer on the snow surface or on a ski pole lying on the snow. These methods only indicate the angle at one small spot and are an inaccurate way to measure the true slope angle.

❄ <u>Do</u> sight your inclinometer to wherever a slope change occurs, preferably shooting a relatively long span of distance. Sight to a point approximately the same elevation above the surface as your eye. Take multiple measurements to corroborate and confirm your findings.

❄ Because every slope is made up of steeper and less steep components, try to measure both ends of the range. Pay attention not to the average, but to the steepest angles. If you travel in the area regularly, record the data for future reference.

This avalanche initially fractured on the steepest (49°) portion of the slope (right side of the top photograph). Then, as is common, it stepped down to a deeper weak layer and propagated onto the lower angle (30°) slope on the left. This part of the 5 foot (1.5 m) fracture is shown in greater detail below.

SLOPE ASPECT (ORIENTATION)

What direction is the slope facing relative to both recent winds and the sun? Subtle changes in slope aspect can greatly affect snow stability. **Be suspicious of leeward, that is, wind-loaded slopes because the deposition of wind-transported snow rapidly increases the stress on the snowpack and enhances slab formation.** You may find that the snow on a slope that is consistently wind-loaded throughout the winter is very homogenous and well-bonded, but you need to check it out! Cornices also develop on leeward aspects and make very effective triggers when they hit the slope below. Given two identical avalanche paths, one with cornices in the starting zone and the other without, the corniced path will produce avalanches with greater frequency and the avalanches will tend to be larger.

The skier who was killed in this avalanche did not recognize the significance of recent wind-loading. Note that there is no snow on the windward side of the ridge. The snow on the leeward side was as hollow-sounding as a drum and it was easy to push a ski pole down through consolidated, fresh wind slab into very soft, weak, sugary snow. Note also the typically variable thickness of the slab along the flank. The skier triggered the slide a few turns into his descent where the slab was thinner and his body weight was able to more easily affect the weak layer.

Slope aspect in relation to the sun is important because while moderate warming can help strengthen and stabilize the snowpack, intense direct sun can have the opposite effect. Furthermore, the snow is often more unstable on shadowed slopes because of generally colder conditions due to the absence of solar warming during much of the winter.

TERRAIN ROUGHNESS (ANCHORING)

Boulders, trees, and ledges act as anchors and can help hold the snow in place *until* the anchors themselves are buried. A grassy slope might avalanche very early in the season with a total snow cover of only an inch or two while a slope covered

The weak layer that lurked on this slope did not exist on the ridge (where it had likely been destroyed by wind) or on other aspects that had received more solar warming. In high latitude areas, most slopes (regardless of aspect) are essentially shadowed in mid-winter because the sun's low angle of incidence means that the slopes receive very little solar input. The avalanche savvy person who intentionally triggered this slope was on the lookout for this layer because he had been monitoring recent weather. He was very careful not to descend too far down the slope so that the avalanche could not break above him.

with large boulders or tree stumps might require deeper snow. Slopes with anchors are less likely to avalanche than open slopes, but the bad news is that anchors (including trees) have to be too closely spaced together for a person to easily travel through to ensure that an avalanche cannot occur. Coniferous (evergreen) trees tend to break up slab continuity because their cone shape encourages sluffing during storms, which helps compact the snow around them. While spacing is the most critical issue, all things being equal, conifers tend to be more effective anchors than deciduous trees.

Note that although all these slopes have similar angles, the one on the right did not avalanche. Why not? While the stairs provided anchoring, as soon as the snow depth increases and they are buried, they will no longer function as effective anchors. Also note the impressive debris piles produced by these small slopes. (Photo by Don Bachman)

The anchoring ability of a slope refers not only to the terrain roughness, but also to the old snow surface. How well do you think the next layer of snow will bond to these icy, smooth slopes, particularly if the storm comes in windless and cold so that the new snowfall is light and fluffy?

The downside of anchors is that they are commonly areas of stress concentration—the snow upslope of them is being held in place while the snow below or to the sides is being pulled downhill by gravity. For this reason, fracture lines often rip between anchor points. Furthermore, as discussed in the snowpack section, rocks and bushes can be "gardens" for the development of weak snow. Thus, the snowpack is sometimes more easily triggered in these areas.

This sparsely treed, 40° slope triggered by a snowmobiler had no problem producing a fracture that ran between anchors.

SLOPE SHAPE

Avalanches can happen on any snow-covered slope steep enough to slide. On convex slopes, slabs are most likely to fracture just below the bulge where stresses are greatest. However, if the snow is highly unstable, it is not uncommon for the failure to propagate upslope, producing a fracture line above this rollover. On broad, smooth (planar) slopes, avalanches can happen anywhere. Slabs often fracture above and below cliff bands.

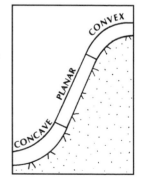

Small concave slopes can provide a small amount of compressive support at the base of the hollow, thus inhibiting slab release, particularly if the slabs are strong and the slopes are not very high (i.e., less than about 25 feet or 7.5 meters). On larger concave slopes, there is not sufficient compressive support to be able to withstand the stresses associated with the steeper slopes above. The bottom line is that all concave slopes are capable of avalanching and it is difficult to predict where the fracture line will break.

Slope shape also influences the flow characteristics of an avalanche (such as velocity and type of motion) as well as the depth and distribution of debris. Beware of terrain traps, that is, steep slopes that end in dips, v-shaped creek bottoms, cliffs, or ravines. Deposition in these areas (even from small avalanches) is is likely to be deep and the consequences of entrapment are usually serious. Slopes that run out onto alluvial fans or gentle, open slopes tend to produce shallower, more widespread debris deposits.

Slabs often fracture just below a convexity where the angle is steeper. Note that in the avalanche pictured, the slope angle below the fracture line is 49° and above, it is only 29°. When the instability is very tender, however, it is not uncommon for avalanches to break above the rollover or even to pull snow off of a flat ridge. Be very careful when dropping over convexities–with every step, the slope angle can increase 2 to 3 degrees.

VEGETATIVE INDICATORS OF AVALANCHE ACTIVITY

Vegetation can provide evidence of the frequency and magnitude of past avalanche occurrences, thus indicating potential avalanche terrain as well as the capability of a given path.

Vegetative indicators include:

✳ swaths of open slope between forested or vegetated areas;

✳ trees that are bent, broken, or uprooted, "broomed" trees (i.e., previously broken but with new growth tops), and vegetation that is polished or "flagged" (i.e., missing branches on the uphill side). Flagging can also indicate the flow height of the avalanches that have impacted the area;

This "flagged" tree, with broken branches on the uphill side, provides information about the frequency and flow heights of avalanches in this path. Note the snow pasted against the trunk indicating the powderblast height of a recent slide.

✳ the presence of "disaster species" such as alders, willows, dwarf birch, aspen, and cottonwoods;

✳ a marked difference in the height of trees (e.g., smaller in the center of the path and larger on the edges).

ELEVATION

Temperature, wind, and precipitation often vary significantly with altitude. Common differences are rain at lower altitude with snow at higher elevations, or variations in precipitation amounts or wind speed with altitude. Generally, upper elevation areas are subjected to greater amounts of snowfall, stronger winds, and colder temperatures (except during periods of inversions). Do not assume that conditions at one elevation will reflect those at another.

PATH HISTORY: IF AN AVALANCHE PATH COULD TALK

Every avalanche path has a history. It is not a question of *if* the path will produce an avalanche, but rather *when*, under what conditions, and how big. Learn as much as you can about the path history of the area where you are traveling, not only by seeking clues at the site but also by communicating with knowledgeable travelers, avalanche forecasters, park rangers, locals, etc. Note, however, that many of the smaller paths or terrain traps most likely to catch travelers are often overlooked. Additionally, be aware that the period of human observation is very short in relation to the life of an avalanche path and our memories are imperfect. Just because a path isn't known to have avalanched does not mean that it has not produced avalanches in the past or will not do so again. Irrationally, recreationists will often shy away from a slope known to have once produced a fatal avalanche, only to go play on an adjacent slope with exactly the same characteristics. The only difference is that the latter slope has not yet earned a reputation or been named for the person who died there.

* * * * *

If the answer to the question, *Is the terrain capable of producing an avalanche?* is "yes," then you either need to go where the answer is "no" or tackle the critical weather and snowpack questions.

Path history may not always be evident, particularly in small paths or those above treeline. The skiers circled in the top photo may not be aware of the runout potential of the slope above them. The same slope is pictured in the bottom photograph. Both avalanches below were triggered simultaneously by a snowmobiler riding on the low angle terrain between the two hills.

WEATHER

Is the Weather
Contributing to Instability?

Most *natural* avalanches occur during or shortly after storms. Weather primes the snowpack for avalanching both by shaping the strength of the existing layers and by adding stress. Let's consider the influence of precipitation, wind, and temperature upon snow stability.

PRECIPITATION (Type, amount, duration, intensity)

The significance of precipitation is that it increases the stress exerted upon the snowpack by adding weight. How much weight is added depends upon the amount of new precipitation and its water content. Low density powder will weigh much less than an equivalent amount of dense, wet snow. While new snow increases stress, it can also provide a certain amount of strength to the snowpack through whatever bonding is taking place.

Rain, on the other hand, adds weight without adding strength until refreezing occurs. Rain can cause rapid weakening by melting the bonds between grains and introducing free water that further erodes the bonding within and between layers. A cold, dry snowpack that has never been rained on is particularly sensitive to even small amounts of rain and will tend to produce avalanches very quickly. Snowpacks that have already been subjected to multiple rain events generally require greater amounts of rain to become unstable. Though a wet snowpack may be very unstable, it tends to strengthen and stabilize rapidly when refrozen. The resulting ice crust can make a classic bed or sliding surface for future snowfalls.

The surface rain runnels above are indicative of a snowpack that has been subjected to heavy amounts of rain. As the rain penetrates into the snowpack, it often forms percolation columns (below) that channel the water downward until a denser layer causes the water to pool. When frozen, the percolation columns act like rebar in concrete and help tie the snow structure together. Once refrozen, such snowpacks are quite strong.

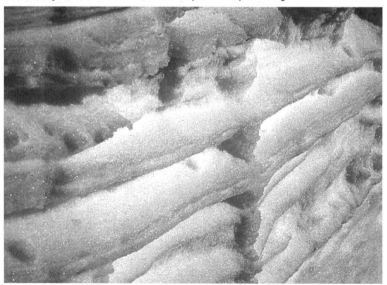

How well the new snow layer bonds to the old snow surface is as important as the type and amount of precipitation that falls. Generally, rough, pitted, irregular surfaces allow for better adhesion to new snow than do smooth, glassy surfaces. Wet, warm, and dense snow will usually bond better than cold, dry snow to any type of surface, even to crusts.

No stock answer exists concerning how much precipitation is required to create instability and cause subsequent avalanching. Some storms drop several feet of new snow with little or no avalanche activity, while others bring just a few inches of new snow but result in widespread activity. This depends, in part, on the bonding qualities of the new snow as well as on the strength of the layers within the snowpack. Generally, however, the most common cause of natural avalanches is increased load due to heavy amounts of precipitation or deposition of wind-transported snow.

The way that the snowpack responds to load depends largely upon the intensity of the force (i.e., amount of loading) and the rate at which it is applied. The more rapid the loading, the less time the snowpack has to adjust to additional stress. In fact, any sudden changes can be a stress on the snowpack. All things being equal, two feet (.6 meters) of new snow falling in ten hours is more likely to create unstable conditions than two feet of new snow falling over three days. Add wind and the problem is rapidly compounded.

WIND (Direction, speed, duration)

It might be a blue sky day but as far as the mountains are concerned, a storm is occurring if the wind is transporting snow. Wind is able to deposit snow roughly ten times faster than it can fall from the sky. It scours windward terrain while rapidly loading leeward slopes and creating cornices. Because the wind breaks down snow crystals as they are bounced along the snow surface, wind-transported snow generally forms compact, often hollow-sounding, cohesive layers. Depending upon wind speed and direction, the consistency of this snow can be soft or hard, but either way, it typically makes good slab material.

Wind speed and direction determine which slopes are being loaded. For instance, southeasterly winds will predominantly load north and west-facing terrain. However, some loading will occur on all aspects as terrain features cause the wind to decelerate and drop snow. Wind-loading commonly occurs in several ways. Top-loading takes place when the wind blows over the top of a ridge, depositing snow just below ridge level. Generally, the stronger the wind, the further downslope the snow is deposited. Side-loading occurs when the wind blows across a slope, loading snow on the leeward side of vertical ribs and in all of the gullies vertically bisecting the slope. Side-loading, also known as cross-loading, is sometimes more insidious because it can be harder to detect, especially in areas of gentle depressions. Furthermore, within an avalanche path that has been side-loaded, there may be greater amounts of snow from top to bottom that can be incorporated into the avalanche, thus increasing the volume and power of the slide.

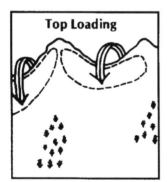 Top Loading

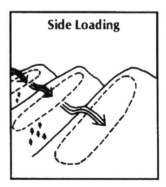 Side Loading

Note that while leeward slopes are becoming potentially more unstable due to increasing load, the stress on windward slopes is decreasing as the snow is stripped off. For this reason, windward slopes often make good routes. Beware though because wind shifts in the mountains are common. Yesterday's windward slope may be wind-loaded today.

The wind threshold speed, that is, the wind speed required to transport snow is largely dependent upon the type of snow at the surface. For example, eight inches (20 centimeters) of loose, unconsolidated powder subjected to 15-20 mile per hour winds (7.5-10 meters/second) would likely create highly unstable snow conditions within a couple of hours due to rapid loading of leeward slopes. However, little transport and thus, little change in stability would occur if the snow surface consisted of a hard-packed old wind slab or an ice crust, even if the wind blew much harder. While snow structure and the size of the upwind area determine the amount of snow available for transport, the intensity and duration of the wind affect the amount and rate of loading.

Wind is often responsible for changing snow stability within minutes or in just a few steps. In the bottom photo, note the sudden transition between wind-eroded snow on the left and the 3 foot (.9 m) drift to the right.

TEMPERATURE (Air temperature trends, snow temperature, solar/terrestrial radiation)

Air temperature trends during a storm are important because they affect layer strength and bonding. Storms that start out cold and get progressively warmer are more likely to produce avalanches than those that start out warm and progressively become cooler. The fluffy cold snow that falls early in the storm often bonds poorly to the old snow surface and is not strong enough to support the denser snow deposited on top of it as temperatures warm. Conversely, relatively warm snow falling at temperatures of roughly high 20's to low 30's°F (-3 to 1°C) often bonds well to the previously warmed old snow surface. However, any rapid, prolonged rise in temperature to above freezing following periods of cold weather may promote instability.

Snow temperature, not to be confused with air temperature, is the regulator for change within the snowpack. **The warmer the snowpack, the more rapidly changes occur within it**, including metamorphism (changes in layer texture and strength) and deformation (compression and downslope flow). As with any change, the faster and/or more intense the warming, the more likely it is to result in avalanching.

A warm layer of new snow (above roughly 28°F or -2°C, but below freezing) will ordinarily settle (compress) rapidly, becoming denser and stronger. Periods of cloudy, moderately warm weather will encourage this settlement process and typically lead to greater snow stability in the long run. Avalanches may, however, occur in the interim—warming can enhance slab formation and also increase the rate of downslope deformation in affected layers. Because layers of different temperatures and densities flow downhill at different rates of speed (warm, less dense layers flow faster), increased stress may result at the interface between warmed snow and colder layers underneath. Layers that have been warmed to the melting point (32°F/0°C) weaken rapidly but also tend to stabilize quickly (often within hours) when cooling temperatures cause refreezing. In a cold snowpack, unstable snow conditions often persist longer, sometimes for weeks or months, because the settlement or strengthening process is slowed. **The bottom line is that instabilities within the snowpack tend to be more short-lived at warmer temperatures and more persistent at colder temperatures.**

Temperatures within the snowpack are influenced by air temperature but they are also a function of the amount of incoming solar (short wave) radiation and of outgoing terrestrial (long wave) radiation, that is, heat being radiated from earth back into the atmosphere. The amount of solar radiation absorbed by the snow surface depends upon the time of day and year, extent of cloud cover, latitude, moisture content of the snowpack, and very importantly, the aspect, elevation, and angle of the slope. Dry snowpacks typically reflect up to 90% of incoming solar radiation while moist or wet snowpacks are capable of absorbing more heat and reflecting less back. Because wet snow is a better solar collector, it is capable of warming faster.

If you have stood on the snow surface on a sunny, winter day, you have likely experienced the sensation of having freezing, tingling toes while your face is pleasantly warm. Cooled by long wave (terrestrial) radiation loss, the snow surface can be many degrees colder than the air just a few feet above. The net cooling of the snow surface can be considerable, particularly on clear nights when there is no incoming solar radiation to offset the escape of long wave radiation into the sky. The resulting steep differences in temperature within the near surface snow layers encourage the development of potentially serious weak layers of facets as discussed in the section on snow metamorphism. Cloud cover, functioning much like a blanket, inhibits heat loss by absorbing and then re-emitting the long wave radiation back towards earth. This means that the snowpack can actually warm more rapidly in cloudy, warm conditions than under sunny skies at the same temperature.

If the winter's snowpack is able to warm gradually, for example, under conditions of temperate days and clear, cold nights that allow the snowpack to regain strength through refreezing, avalanche activity will typically be limited to warmed surface layers releasing later in the day. These layers peel off (much like an onion skin) in the form of loose snow slides and shallow slabs. Even when small, the debris in these slides can be much like a slurry of concrete and harden similarly. Cornice breaks are also possible under these conditions. Given buried weak layers or discontinuities in the snowpack, prolonged warming can result in deeper slab releases, especially after several consecutive nights when the snowpack does not refreeze. It is typical for some of these deep slab instabilities to be triggered by warming-induced loose snow slides or cornice breaks.

When dealing with a snowpack that is being subjected to significant warming, timing is critical. A slope that is hard and stable in the morning may produce avalanches by the afternoon as upper layer ice crusts are transformed into wet snow. Remember that a rapidly warming snowpack also weakens very rapidly. Traveling in springtime conditions is an art because it is easy to miss the short window between, for example, sensational, steep terrain skiing or boarding in 2 or 3 inches (5-8 cm) of warmed snow (commonly called corn snow) and potentially deadly travel in very weak, ankle deep slush. Early signs that the snowpack in a given area is warming include a cupping texture on the snow surface and snowballs (also called sunballs) rolling downslope. These clues do not necessarily mean that a slope has to be avoided but it is critical to monitor how fast the warming is penetrating into the snowpack. Note that avalanche activity often peaks several hours after the daily peak in solar radiation.

Sunballs (evident on the lower slope) indicate surface instability due to solar warming but tell nothing about what might be happening deeper in the snowpack. This clue is significant as an indicator of change and it is important to monitor how rapidly the snowpack is warming. Though the higher slope has the same aspect, no sunballs are present. Apparently, no temperature inversion exists and colder temperatures at higher elevations have offset the effects of solar warming.

Remember that the absence of warming on a slope throughout much of the winter can be as potentially hazardous as direct, intense sun. Shaded slopes are prime habitat for early season avalanche accidents because they tend to accumulate snow earliest and colder conditions favor the development of weak layers. Instabilities are also likely to linger longer than on other aspects, often persisting well into the spring.

By anticipating the effects of weather conditions and changing weather patterns upon the snowpack, you can vastly increase your margin of safety when traveling in avalanche terrain.

TYPICAL WEATHER PATTERNS RESULTING IN UNSTABLE SNOW CONDITIONS AND AVALANCHE ACTIVITY

❄ **Heavy amount of new snow loading in a short period.** *Result:* Increased stress due to rapid loading.

❄ **Rain.** *Result:* Weight but no strength is added to the snowpack. Bonds between grains are eroded and weakened. Cold, dry snowpacks that have never been rained on require only small amounts of rain to become unstable.

❄ **Long cold, clear, calm period followed by heavy precipitation and/or wind-loading.** *Result:* Deposition of a slab over one or more weak layers (probably well-developed layers of faceted grains or hoar frost).

❄ **Storms that start out cold and end warm.** Or warm storms with temperatures near the freezing level that follow long periods (several days or weeks) of cold weather. *Result:* Development of an "upside-down layer cake." Instability is generally high but short-lived.

❄ **Winds causing significant snow transport.** *Result:* Rapid loading of leeward slopes, development of wind slabs, and cornice formation. Add a layer of powder snow over the slabs making them more difficult to detect and the probability of human-triggered avalanches becomes even higher.

❄ **Rapid and prolonged temperature rise to above freezing after a period of cold weather.** *Result:* If the snowpack was previously stable, some surface instability may occur until temperatures cool. If weak layers exist within the snowpack, deeper slab releases are possible and may be triggered by cornice collapses or loose snow slides.

❄ **Intense solar radiation on days near or above freezing.** *Result:* Shallow loose snow and slab avalanches may occur as surface layer(s) weaken rapidly (especially if a thin veil of cloud cover exists). If deeper instabilities are present, deep slab avalanches could be triggered, particularly during prolonged springtime warming

Could the Snow Slide?

SNOWPACK LAYERING AND BONDING

No two storms are exactly alike. Each new snow or wind event creates a different layer or sometimes, several layers in the snowpack. Once on the ground, the layers are subject to changes in texture and strength throughout the winter. These changes help determine snow strength by influencing how well individual snow grains are bonded to each other, both within a layer and between layers. Within any given snowpack, there are stronger and weaker layers. Strong layers tend to be made up of well-bonded, small, rounded grains. Weak layers are composed of poorly bonded or cohesionless grains. A thin weak layer or discontinuity can be created simply if one layer is poorly bonded to another.

Many combinations of strong and weak layers can exist within the snowpack. The structure of the snowpack varies greatly depending upon the particular season, specific location, and regional snow climate. Even on a small slope, the distribution and characteristics of snow layers may differ within a short distance (sometimes just a few feet), often due to subtle changes in slope aspect, angle, shape, snow depth, and underlying ground surface.

Do not be misled by the terms weak and strong. Strong does not necessarily mean stable. A strong layer is cohesive enough to fracture as a slab. What is important is the *relative* cohesiveness of the layers. **Slab avalanche potential exists when relatively strong, cohesive snow overlies weaker snow or is not bonded well to the underlying layer.**

A common misconception is to assume that cohesive snow is something solid that you can pick up in chunks. Cohesive snow can be soft,

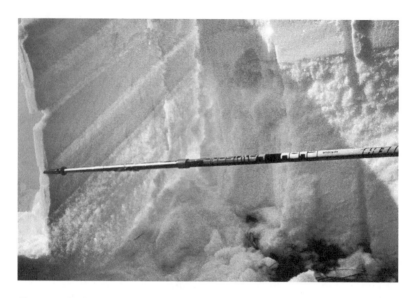

The strength of the layers within the snowpack is subject to change throughout the winter. In the top photograph, note the stronger (darker) and weaker (lighter) layers clearly evident in the sidewall of a pit that is being backlit by the sun. Similar variability in layer structure and thickness can be seen in the fracture line below.

powdery snow that you almost need a snorkel to travel through or can be very hard, wind-deposited snow that is difficult to kick toeholds into. **Snow that is cohesive enough to fracture and avalanche is potential slab material, regardless of hardness.**

Snow metamorphism is the name given to describe the changes in structure that take place over time within the snowpack. There are several types of snow metamorphism. Each occurs under a different set of conditions and as discussed, each affects the strength of the snowpack. As conditions change, the dominant type of metamorphism in a given layer may change. Also importantly, different types of metamorphism may be occurring in various layers of the snowpack at the same time. The rate or speed of the metamorphic process is strongly dependent on the temperature of a given snow layer. The colder the temperature, the slower the rate of change.

Whether you remember the different types of metamorphism or can definitively identify different types of snow grains is unimportant. What is critical is that you are able to recognize relatively strong and, especially, weak layers in the field. However, if you do learn something about the conditions that produce different kinds of layers (i.e., potential slabs, weak layers, and bed or sliding surfaces), you will be better able to anticipate the stability of the snowpack before you even reach the trailhead. If you want to learn more about snow metamorphism, read on. If not, skip to the next section.

MORE ABOUT SNOW METAMORPHISM

The mechanism for causing any kind of snow metamorphism is the movement of water molecules. Water is the only substance on the planet that exists in nature as a liquid, solid, and vapor. One reason that snow is such a unique and dynamic material is that all three phases occur within the snowpack. While snow appears to be a solid white blanket, it is actually an ice skeleton that contains mostly air. Newly fallen powder might be as much as 95% air while the air content of snow that has been on the ground for some time may be closer to 60 or 70 percent. The air within the snowpack has a relative humidity near 100%, which means that dry snow consists of both ice and water vapor. In wet snow, liquid water is also present.

The two types of metamorphism that take place in cold, dry snow are rounding and faceting. The presence or absence of a significant *temperature gradient*, that is, a difference in temperature across a given distance, determines whether rounded or faceted grains develop within a layer. A third type of metamorphism is known as melt-freeze.

Rounded grains develop when the temperature in a layer or between layers is nearly uniform, that is, there is only a small, insignificant temperature gradient. While individual grains become smaller and rounder, bonds or necks between grains are developed. This bonding process is known as *sintering* and increases the layer strength. Thus,

If you magnified a thin section of this hard wind slab, you would see fine, rounded grains as shown in the inset. Note the necks or bonds between grains that help make this such a cohesive layer. (Inset photo from John Montagne collection)

the rounding process produces fine, rounded, well-bonded grains and the result is a relatively strong layer, with moderate to high density. Remember not to confuse the terms strong and stable. Strong snow makes good slab material because it is cohesive enough to be able to fracture.

Favorable conditions for the development of rounded grains are cloudy, mild weather and/or a thick snowpack. Every metamorphic process has an early, intermediate, and advanced stage. The longer the rounding process continues in a given layer, the more advanced the grains—that is, the individual grains become smaller as the bonds between them are enhanced.

Faceted grains develop when a significant temperature gradient exists within or between layers. In most areas, the temperature at the ground/snow interface is warmer than the air temperature. Shallower snowpacks or colder air temperatures result in greater temperature gradients within the snowpack. Deep snowpacks tend to dampen this difference by adding many layers of insulation between the relatively warm ground and cold air. So what is a significant temperature gradient? In regions where the average snowpack temperature is close to 0°C or 32°F, a significant gradient is 1°C per 10 centimeters (1.8°F per 4 inches). In very cold areas such as the Canadian Rockies or interior Alaska, where the average snowpack temperature is usually much colder than 0°C, it takes a larger gradient to drive the faceting process.

Faceting produces large, angular grains that are poorly bonded and weak. The longer the gradient exists and the process continues, the larger, more faceted, and more persistent the grains. Because faceted grains have much the same consistency as granular sugar, they are sometimes referred to as sugar snow. Advanced faceted grains are also known as "depth hoar." Faceted snow is often the layer that collapses and goes "whumph" as you travel across the snow surface. It is particularly sensitive as a weak layer when subjected to significant loading of new or wind-transported snow.

Faceted grains, in any stage of development, can be a potential weak layer although there is a tendency to focus on the large, cupped, advanced facets or depth hoar crystals shown above. In the 14 inch (36 cm) fracture line below, the slab was made up of early facets, the weak layer of intermediate facets, and the bed surface of advanced facets. What was important was that the slab was relatively cohesive compared to the underlying snow. The entire snowpack was only knee deep and was so soft that every step easily penetrated to the ground. This was one of the most sensitive instabilities we have ever seen—avalanches could be triggered a considerable distance away from the slopes and were releasing on slope angles as low as 26.5°. As cold weather and the resulting temperature gradient persisted, the whole snowpack developed into advanced facets. Though some loose snow slides occurred, there were no further slab avalanches until the next storm deposited a slab and produced widespread activity. (Top photo by Bill Glude)

While the large depth hoar at the bottom of many snowpacks may be most obvious, do not ignore the facets that can fom near the snow surface and create dangerous avalanche conditions once buried. In fact, these "near-surface facets" are responsible for more avalanche accidents than depth hoar. Periods of clear weather with mild, sunny days and cold nights create strong temperature gradients near the snow surface—ideal conditions for producing faceted grains. Because the process makes the snow less cohesive, often improving the skiing and riding conditions, some call it recycled powder. Strong near-surface temperature gradients can also develop around layers saturated by rain or melted by the sun as they begin to refreeze. Near-surface facets can be created in a few hours or a few days. Though the grains may not develop into obvious cupped facets like depth hoar, they will still be uncohesive, angular, poorly bonded, and could be very tender when the next load of new or windblown snow is deposited.

Favorable conditions for developing faceted grains are cold weather and/or a thin snowpack. Also, because temperature gradients are enhanced on either side of ice crusts or very dense layers, faceted grains are often observed at these interfaces. Facets form more readily in low density (high porosity) snow because the temperature gradient in more widely spaced grains is larger and the grains have room to grow. Conversely, if a temperature gradient is introduced within a hard wind slab made up of small, rounded grains, faceting will take over as the driving type of metamorphism, but it is unlikely that any substantial change in structure will occur because the snow is too dense. Perhaps you have had the unexpected treat of suddenly plunging deep into the snowpack when you are near rocks, tree wells, or bushes. Chances are you've just found sugar snow. These are "garden" spots for faceted grains to develop because they often have greater temperature gradients and large air spaces.

As mentioned, advanced faceted grains will persist as an obvious discontinuity long after the temperature gradient has dissipated and the rounding process has established itself in the layer (thus causing grains to round somewhat). Once depth hoar forms, it is likely to remain in the snowpack for the rest of the winter. It can be eliminated if the slope avalanches to the ground and then a series of storms quickly deposits enough new snow to insulate the warm ground from the cool air, thus preventing a temperature gradient from developing and a new weak layer from forming. Another way to eliminate depth hoar is if heavy rain percolates into the layer and then refreezes. If the depth hoar does persist, avalanching may or may not occur depending on whether stress is increased, incrementally or at once, to critical levels. Avalanches to the ground and whumphing (collapsing) noises are bull's-eye clues that the depth hoar is sensitive.

Melt form or melt-freeze grains develop when meltwater or rain enters the snowpack and the snowpack temperature reaches 0°C (32°F). Melt-freeze metamorphism happens on warm, sun-exposed slopes, during mid-winter thaws, or in spring. The trend is toward the production of coarse, rounded grains. With repeated cycles of melting and refreezing, these grains become larger and larger (and are often called corn snow). In the freeze phase, the grains are well-bonded and strong. The resulting ice crusts can, however, make good potential bed surfaces for slabs subsequently formed on top of them. In the melt phase, the smaller grains and the necks between grains begin to melt and weaken rapidly. This is why timing is so important in the spring near steep slopes that are being subjected to warming.

There are other important weak layers. *Surface hoar or hoar frost*, the wintertime equivalent of summertime dew, is formed at the snow surface during cold, clear weather. Surface hoar crystals are loose, feathery, and poorly bonded. Surface hoar is a potentially deadly weak layer once buried because it persists for a relatively long period of time (commonly 3-6 weeks, sometimes months), can be very thin and difficult to detect even if you are looking for it, and can produce long-running fracture lines. It also tends to avalanche on relatively low slope angles (i.e., often at or below 36°) and is a very sensitive layer that can be triggered a long distance away from the slope. Slab

Melt form grains such as those above are formed after repeated cycles of melting and freezing. Rain can accelerate this process and produce wet avalanches like the one pictured below.

fractures on surface hoar tend to rip well above the rollovers on convexities and may even arc right up onto a flat ridge.

Surface hoar is responsible for a large percentage of avalanche fatalities. However, the conditions leading up to the problem can be quite obvious. For example, picture yourself bemoaning the lack of recent snowfall, yet traveling along through delightful, "tinkly-sounding" hoar frost. The next week there is a large dump of new snow. Rather

Surface hoar, though delicate in structure, can persist as a potentially unstable shear plane for weeks or months. Note that the weak layer of surface hoar is still evident even after it was overrun by the shallow wind slab pictured. The skier who triggered this slide missed several key clues: a long, cold, clear period followed by new snow and little wind until the end of the storm (this is significant because the surface hoar was buried rather than being destroyed by rain or wind), steep slope angle, and fresh wind slab texture on this lee slope. The large surface hoar crystals in the inset photograph are roughly a half inch (1.3 cm) wide.

than jumping onto the slopes with abandon, head out into the mountains with "avalanche eyeballs," anticipating that the buried surface hoar might be a serious problem. Remember that surface hoar is a persistent weak layer and do not forget to keep monitoring it long after it is buried.

Another potential weak layer is *unmetamorphosed new snow*. This is snow that may have fallen during a cool or windless period of a storm and then had denser, heavier snow deposited on top of it. Still another is *graupel*, a type of precipitation. These rounded, styrofoam-like icy pellets often roll downslope (particularly when deposited on a hard snow surface) and collect in depressions or at the bottom of steep slopes and cliff bands, thus forming areas that may be more trigger sensitive once the next load is deposited. While both of these weak layers produce avalanches, they tend to stabilize within a few days and do not typically form persistent snowpack weaknesses.

Rounded grains often make up slabs while faceted grains form classic weak layers. However, as shown in an earlier photograph, slab avalanches have occurred in which the slabs were composed of early faceted grains, the weak layer of intermediate facets, and the bed surface of advanced facets or depth hoar. On the other hand, if the entire snowpack is composed of a homogenous layer of faceted snow (i.e., equally uncohesive, with no structural discontinuities), there is little or no potential for slab release under most circumstances although loose snow releases may occur. Any layer can be a bed surface, even very soft, powdery snow, so it is usually best to focus attention on potential slab and weak layers.

Remember that what is critical in terms of snow stability is the relative cohesiveness of the layers and how well they are bonded to each other.

SNOW METAMORPHISM SUMMARY

● *ROUNDS*

    CONDITIONS
- Lack of a significant temperature gradient
- Cloudy, warm weather
- Thick snowpack

    SIGNIFICANCE

Strong (note that strong does not necessarily equal stable), well-bonded layer, classic slab material

☐ *FACETS*

    CONDITIONS
- Significant temperature gradient
- Shallow snowpack
- Cold, clear weather
- On shadowed aspects
- Lower density, more porous snow
- Near snow surface
- Around crusts
- Near rocks, trees

    SIGNIFICANCE

Weak, poorly bonded layer (early, intermediate, and advanced stages of development), collapsible, sensitive, persistent

○ *MELT FORM*

    CONDITIONS

Melting/freezing temperatures
Rain or warm weather

    SIGNIFICANCE

Freeze = strong (but crust can be good future sliding surface)
Melt = weak (rapid weakening, free water lubrication)

TYPICAL UNSTABLE SNOW STRUCTURES IN DRY SNOW*

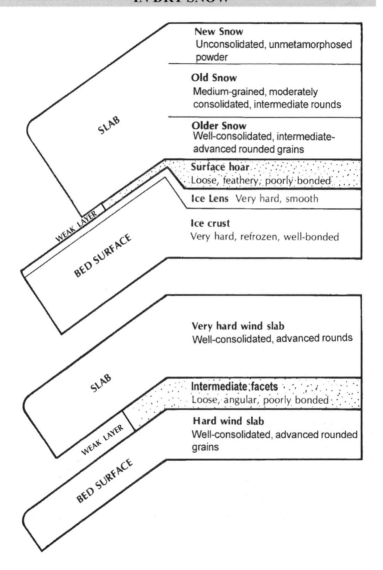

New Snow
Unconsolidated, unmetamorphosed powder

Old Snow
Medium-grained, moderately consolidated, intermediate rounds

Older Snow
Well-consolidated, intermediate-advanced rounded grains

Surface hoar
Loose, feathery, poorly bonded

Ice Lens Very hard, smooth

Ice crust
Very hard, refrozen, well-bonded

SLAB

WEAK LAYER

BED SURFACE

Very hard wind slab
Well-consolidated, advanced rounds

Intermediate facets
Loose, angular, poorly bonded

Hard wind slab
Well-consolidated, advanced rounded grains

SLAB

WEAK LAYER

BED SURFACE

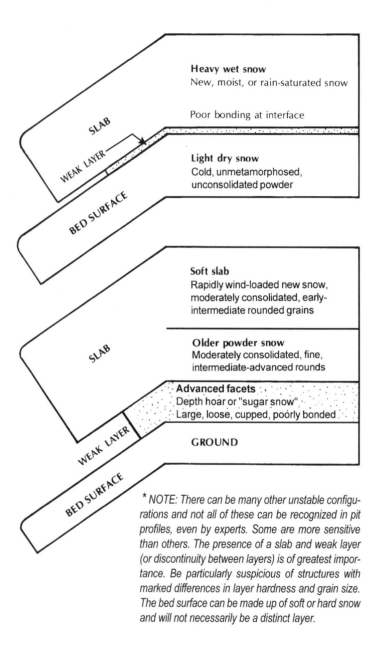

Heavy wet snow
New, moist, or rain-saturated snow

Poor bonding at interface

SLAB

WEAK LAYER

BED SURFACE

Light dry snow
Cold, unmetamorphosed,
unconsolidated powder

Soft slab
Rapidly wind-loaded new snow,
moderately consolidated, early-
intermediate rounded grains

Older powder snow
Moderately consolidated, fine,
intermediate-advanced rounds

SLAB

Advanced facets
Depth hoar or "sugar snow"
Large, loose, cupped, poorly bonded

WEAK LAYER

GROUND

BED SURFACE

*NOTE: There can be many other unstable configu-
rations and not all of these can be recognized in pit
profiles, even by experts. Some are more sensitive
than others. The presence of a slab and weak layer
(or discontinuity between layers) is of greatest importance. Be particularly suspicious of structures with
marked differences in layer hardness and grain size.
The bed surface can be made up of soft or hard snow
and will not necessarily be a distinct layer.

DEFORMATION: HOW SNOW BEHAVES AS A MATERIAL

While metamorphism describes the changes in snow grains, the term *deformation* describes how the variable, interconnected, multi-layered, dynamic, three-dimensional ice skeleton we call a snowpack changes over time. On the flats, where gravity is the only force at work, compression from the weight of the snow causes grains to become more tightly packed and pore spaces to become smaller. This process, called *settlement*, makes snow denser and stronger. Snow layers most susceptible to change are typically new, warm, and low density. As snow settles, it also becomes more resistant to further densification.

On inclined slopes, however, snow doesn't just deform vertically through compression but is constantly flowing downhill through *glide* (the slow motion sliding of the entire snowpack along the ground) and *creep* (a combination of vertical compression and slope parallel flow). When we see snow flowing down a roof and curling over the edge, we are witnessing both processes. Dissimilar snow layers deform at different rates depending upon structure, snow temperature, and the amount and rate of stress applied. This is critical because the interfaces between them often become areas of stress concentration.

Settlement cones around obstacles such as shrubs and rocks are an indicator of how much the snowpack has settled since the last snowfall. What do these cones tell you about the stability of the snowpack? As snow settles, it becomes denser and stronger, but the added cohesiveness may also make it better slab material. It is vital to determine how well the new snow is bonded to underlying layers.

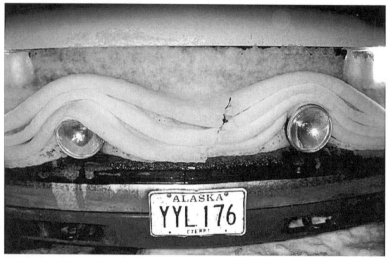

The flowing and bending properties of snow are clearly illustrated on the front of this truck. Note also the brittle fracture between the auxiliary headlights.

When a load is applied slowly or in small increments, the snowpack tends to respond through viscous deformation. Rapid or heavy loading is likely to cause the snowpack to respond in a brittle manner, fracturing and shattering like plate glass. **The key concept to remember is that the snowpack can only adjust to a certain amount of stress and only at a limited rate (intensity).** Stress can be delivered in a variety of ways including new snow load from storms or wind transport, rain events, cornice collapses, significant warming, and human impact.

RECIPE FOR A SLAB AVALANCHE

In the simplest sense, a slab avalanche requires a slab, a weak layer, a slope steep enough to slide, and a trigger. Some combinations of slabs and weak layers are much more sensitive than others, but strong and weak layers are present in almost every snowpack, every season. And though we can be effective triggers, we don't always trigger avalanches. Why not? Several more ingredients are necessary to make the snowpack avalanche.

A condition of *instability* exists when the stress applied to a weak layer is greater than its strength in a localized area and conditions are ripe for fracturing. Much is still being discovered about the fracture mechanics that cause slab release but research indicates that avalanches start as one or more unseen, slope parallel flaws or cracks in the weak layer (*crack initiation*). At that point, if conditions are favorable, the crack will rapidly propagate on its own through the weak layer, extending laterally across the slope (*crack propagation*).

In order to initiate a crack, the stress applied to the weak layer at that area of the slope has to exceed the weak layer strength. The crack must then grow to a critical size, which is on the order of the thickness of the slab. Cracks are commonly initiated by additional load (again both the amount and the rate of loading are key) and, of course, people have proven quite talented at inflicting stress.

If we were able to shrink ourselves down and climb inside the weak layer to watch the process of crack initiation, we would see a few small grains and the bonds between them breaking. This, of course, would increase the stress on the adjoining bonds and grains. If strong enough to hold together, the process will stop. If not strong enough, bond breakage will occur exponentially until the strength of the ice skeleton is overcome and a localized portion of the weak layer collapses catastrophically. This sudden, localized collapse causes the release of stored potential energy, and if the slab is capable of communicating the fracture to the surrounding area, it will result in rapid crack propagation outward in all directions (across the slope and within the weak layer). On an incline, a combination of collapse and shear failure (slope parallel bond breakage) are at work, but collapse plays the major role. Even small and subtle collapses can provide ample energy to drive the fracture process.

Sometimes a crack might initiate in the weak layer but if it doesn't get bigger (i.e., won't propagate), the slope will not avalanche. Other times, the slab and weak layer might be capable of propagation but it may be difficult to initiate the fracture unless the snowpack is tweaked in just the right spot or is impacted by a big trigger such as a large cornice break. Both crack initiation and crack propagation are necessary to get the snowpack to avalanche.

A simple analogy can help explain the process of crack initiation and propagation. Picture an extremely large, but not very well built, two-story parking garage. Brick and wood pillars of questionable strength support the upper floor. Think of the upper story as the slab, the uncertain pillars as the weak layer, and the lower story as the bed surface. If a bulldozer starts to knock the pillars down one-by-one, it will create a larger space in the weak layer (i.e., a flaw or crack), causing further weakening. As the bulldozer continues knocking down pillars, more and more stress will be transferred to the shaky pillars on the outer edges of the "crack." At some point, the crack will reach a critical size, causing the surrounding pillars to collapse on their own. The collapse will then propagate outward rapidly.

All of these avalanches were triggered from the flats in the foreground. A lone skier initiated a collapse that propagated upslope and caused the releases. (Photo by Chris Lundy)

In the same example, imagine what might happen if large trucks were being parked on the top deck even though it had been designed only for lightweight compact cars. As the number of trucks increases, so will the stress exerted on the weak pillars. At some point, one or two pillars will crumble and a "crack" will start to form. This will put even greater stress on the adjoining pillars. If enough load is added, the crack will quickly grow to critical size. Fewer trucks may be needed to cause crack initiation if the load is applied rapidly (i.e., the trucks arrive in quick succession). Once critical size is reached, no additional trucks will be needed. The remaining pillars will collapse, causing widespread fracturing and the entire second floor will fail catastrophically.

The parking garage analogy would be most accurate if we inclined the floors. Remember that even if crack propagation occurs, an avalanche will not release unless the slope is steep enough to overcome residual friction at the bed surface. Again, measurements suggest that this minimum slope angle in cold, dry snow can be as low as 25° though slope angles starting in the low 30s are more commonly observed. At times of high instability, however, cracks in the weak layer may propagate a considerable distance and cause slab fracture on connected steeper slopes.

Avalanches would be much easier to predict and manage if not for the dramatic variability of the snowpack. **It is critically important to note that stress and strength are not evenly distributed across a slope due to terrain and snowpack irregularities.** Slabs vary in depth, density, and distribution, while weak layers differ similarly in thickness, strength, and structural characteristics. As a result of this spatial variability, most slopes have areas where the snowpack is weaker and others that are subjected to greater stress. This means that there are places where a person is more likely to trigger an avalanche (called tender spots or trigger zones), and other locations where triggering an avalanche is more difficult or impossible. *Trigger zones* are prime habitat for crack initiation and propagation. Some call them "sweet spots" but considering the potential consequences, this terminology is misleading—"sour spots" may be more appropriate.

This avalanche was triggered where the snow was thinner and weaker, and then propagated into the much deeper, stronger snow below. Six of seven snowmobilers were caught in the slide and two were killed.

Shallow snowpack areas are likely trigger zones because: 1) they often have more developed weak layers, 2) it is easier for the weight or movement of a person to affect the weak layer and initiate cracks, and 3) cracks are more likely to propagate from shallow areas into deeper, stronger snow than vice versa. However, if the area is too shallow, the slab might not be well developed enough to sustain crack propagation. Other likely trigger zones include the areas around trees, rocks, and bushes (also prime habitat for the development of weak layers of faceted snow) and terrain breaks such as convex rollovers, the edges of gullies or depressions, or wherever the slope is steepest.

Sometimes you will be able to detect the likely trigger zones after an avalanche has already run. Study these carefully as this will help you develop good X-ray vision for snow-covered slopes that have not yet released.

If the conditions on a slope are ripe for fracture propagation, then whether or not a slope is stable depends on how much force is needed to initiate a crack from the weakest part of the slope. A very unstable slope might be triggered by a skier merely approaching the slope's edge. If the snowpack on the same slope is just a bit stronger, it might require two snowmobilers, or one skier falling, or one snowboarder jumping off a cornice, or a couple of climbers kicking steps into a tender spot. There have been accidents where a slope tolerated dozens of recreationists before it released.

Every period of instability has a beginning, a middle, and an end. Somewhere in this continuum exists a period of time where the snow-pack is particularly susceptible to avalanching, provided sufficient stress is applied. Perhaps those first recreationists missed the critical areas where a crack could be initiated and where it could propagate. Or perhaps they negotiated the slope very early or late in the cycle of instability when the snowpack was stronger and required more stress. Or maybe the weak layer just wasn't ready to go until the right combination of placement, timing, and force were applied.

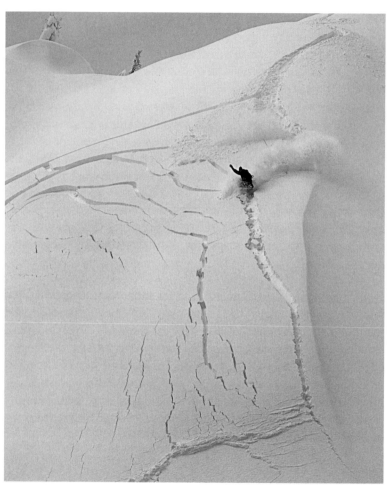

This photo shows all the necessary ingredients for a slab avalanche. First, there is a potentially unstable snowpack consisting of a soft slab (roughly 12 inches or 30 centimeters of new snow) over a weak layer. Second, the snowboarder has added enough stress to initiate a crack within the weak layer. Third, this crack quickly reached critical size, causing the slope to fracture around the rider. Finally, the terrain is clearly steep enough to overcome the residual friction along the bed surface because the slab is beginning to move downslope. Now the rider has only a split second to dig into the bed surface, try to ride it out, or better yet, exit to the relative safety of the subtle ridge on his left. (Photo by Garrett Grove)

Sometimes a slope is so stable that you can drive a herd of elephants across it without triggering an avalanche. If you are determined to make that slope avalanche, maybe 10,000 elephants will do it, but at this point it is becoming a bit academic and it would be more fun to go play in the snow.

EVALUATING SNOW STABILITY

Snow stability evaluation, the process of determining if the snowpack is capable of avalanching, is just a fancy name for "hammering" on the snowpack to see how it responds. It is an ongoing process that, ideally, starts before you arrive in avalanche terrain and continues as long as you are in the mountains, but it does not have to take a lot of time. Remember to begin by formulating an opinion about the stability of the snow before you even head outside. This will help you identify what you know and don't know about what has been happening in the mountains. Always be willing to change your opinion based upon new information.

Remove your blinders by getting off the broken trail frequently. If you are snowmobiling, be sure to turn off your machine periodically, take your helmet off, and walk through the snow. Look, listen, and feel for clues (or lack of clues) to instability. There are almost always clues letting you know how sensitive the snowpack is. Your job is to make sure you don't miss them.

 The bull's-eye snow stability questions are:

❋ **Is there an unstable snow structure (slab/weak layer combination)?**
❋ **If so, what is its depth and distribution?**
❋ **How well are the layers bonded?**
❋ **How much force will it take to make the slope avalanche?**

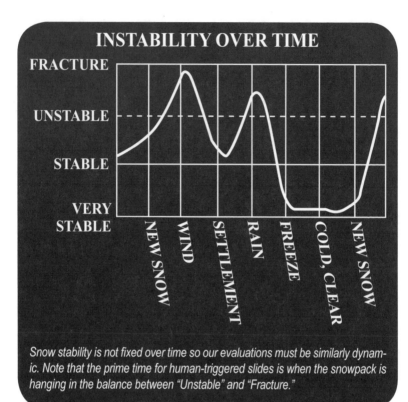

INSTABILITY OVER TIME

FRACTURE

UNSTABLE

STABLE

VERY
STABLE

NEW SNOW · WIND · SETTLEMENT · RAIN · FREEZE · COLD, CLEAR · NEW SNOW

Snow stability is not fixed over time so our evaluations must be similarly dynamic. Note that the prime time for human-triggered slides is when the snowpack is hanging in the balance between "Unstable" and "Fracture."

BULL'S-EYE CLUES TO INSTABILITY INCLUDE:

Recent Avalanche Activity on Similar Slopes

There is no clue more emphatic in its message about avalanche potential than evidence of recent avalanche activity. Avoid slopes of similar angles, aspects, and elevations that have not yet released.

Whumphing Noises

Whumphs are the sounds made when a weak layer (commonly faceted grains, but also surface hoar, unmetamorphosed new snow, and others) collapses within the snowpack. This means that serious instability exists and Nature is literally screaming in your ear! Measure your slope angles carefully. Avoid traveling on slopes steep enough to slide or in runout zones where the collapse you cause could trigger the slopes above you. Whumphs, particularly those that are loud and distinct, often indicate the type of instability that can propagate over a long distance. Note: Some people use the term "settling" instead of collapsing or whumphing. We discourage use of this term as it is too easily confused with the very different settlement process that strengthens the snowpack.

Shooting Cracks

Cracks (localized fractures) radiating out in the snow around you indicate not only that a cohesive slab exists, but also that conditions are favorable for crack propagation. The longer the cracks, the more tender the instability but no matter the length, do not ignore this clue. Some shallow, localized cracking within a narrow radius of a few feet around you may represent less of a threat but still warrants investigation as it is an indicator that the surface layer is acting differently than the layer underneath. It may just be a breakable layer like a crust or it may be a thin slab, poorly bonded to the layer beneath. Pay attention to the depth and distribution of the slab. A slab that is a few inches thick in one spot may be considerably thicker just a short distance across the slope. Be very careful traveling under, on, or near steep snow-filled slopes in these conditions.

Recent Wind-Loading

Evidence of deposition of wind-transported snow includes smooth "pillows," cornices and drift patterns on the snow surface and around obstacles. Such wind-loading increases the stress on the snowpack and greatly enhances slab formation by packing grains of snow together and making them more cohesive.

Snow texture patterns are often a more reliable indicator of recent wind direction than cornices that can build on both sides of a ridge in response to winds from opposite directions. These patterns tell a story of how the snow has been distributed and acted upon by the wind—learn to read them. Constantly scanning ahead for changes in these patterns could prevent you from stumbling onto a wind slab. When deposition has occurred, drift tails point the way the wind is blowing, much like an arrow from a drawn bow.

Tails and rippled patterns will extend from the leeward side of rocks, trees, or across slopes. Erosion causes the snow surface to be undercut on the windward side, with the undercut tail pointing into the wind.

If you see wind pluming (blowing snow) or flat, lenticular clouds indicating strong winds aloft, ask yourself how much snow is available for transport, how much loading is occurring, which slopes are being loaded, and at what rate. Suspect instability on wind-loaded or lee slopes. If you see evidence of snow erosion by wind, think about where the windblown snow was deposited.

Hollow Sounds

These hollow, sometimes drum-like, sounds indicate unstable layering, that is, a less consolidated weak layer overcapped by a denser, stronger layer. Investigate!

These are just some of Nature's clues. **You do not have to see recent avalanches, hear whumphing noises, or have shooting cracks to get caught in an avalanche.** You might only know that there was a recent dump of snow or that the wind was howling. You absolutely will have some combination of clues available to you. Seek them out and listen to their message!

Evidence of recent avalanche activity is the best clue of all regarding potential instability. What kind of avalanches are you seeing? Are the releases isolated or widespread? On what angles, aspects, and at what elevations have they occurred? How deep and wide did they break? How far did they run? Is there a pattern? Note that cornice breaks, slab avalanches, and loose snow slides are all visible in this photograph.

These lenticular winds are indicators of stong winds aloft. Always try to anticipate how the wind, an approaching storm, or other weather variables might affect the stability of the snowpack. (Photo by Nick Parker)

This shooting crack is indisputable evidence that the snowpack is capable of propagating fractures. Long-running, deep cracks like this one indicate especially sensitive snow. Even without such obvious cracking, the rippled snow surface texture is a clue that the wind has been acting on the snow and demands that you know something about how well the layers are bonded. If you miss all of these clues, you might still pick up on the hollow-sounding snow indicating that less dense, weaker snow underlies the wind slab.

Always pay attention to surface texture patterns as indicators of where wind slabs may lurk. When wind deposition occurs, drift tails point the way the wind is blowing. Note that multiple clues—pluming off the ridge, upslope drift tails, cornices, and avalanche activity—all show that the wind has been blowing from left to right.

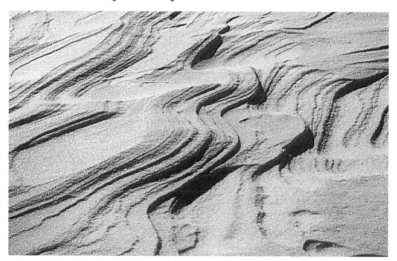

When wind erodes snow, it undercuts it on the windward side. This photo shows erosional features—the wind was blowing from right to left. Where did the windblown snow get deposited? Be suspicious of loading on the next leeward rollover.

MORE ON FIELD TESTS AND OBSERVATIONS

You must knit together the story that the snowpack is trying to tell. Usually, you will find that the various pieces of information back each other up and deliver the same message.

Approach small but steep hills from the top and jump on them to see how they respond. Depending on the instability, you can sometimes get very useful feedback from a slope that is only a few feet high. If you are switchbacking uphill on skis and have just turned a corner, jump just below your uphill ski track and see if you can get a "piece of the pie" to break into blocks, indicating that the snow may be co-hesive enough to propagate a fracture. Regardless of your mode of travel, make a habit of moving a foot or two above the broken track once in a while to see if you can get the undisturbed snow between you and the track to fracture.

Many backcountry travelers have been led to believe that they must dig a snowpit to evaluate snow stability. This is not necessarily true. You may be able to travel for days, weeks, or months, reliably evaluating snow stability by integrating bull's-eye data, without ever digging a pit. Remember that a snowpit is just one piece of information, the quality of which depends greatly on where you choose to dig and how you conduct your tests. Pits can be misleading because snow structure and stability typically vary greatly across any given slope.

Digging a pit is one way of helping to eliminate uncertainty about the layering and bonding of the snowpack at a particular location. It can be especially helpful when traveling in new territory where you are unfamiliar with the season's snow and weather history. Never rely on your snowpit to tell you that the snowpack is stable. Instead, use it as part of your search for instability. Far too many people have died because they gained false confidence from one snowpit and ignored obvious signs of instability.

Do not spend a lot of time in a snowpit. Indeed, it is usually much more useful to quickly integrate data (i.e., observations, clues, and/ or snowpit tests) from a number of locations rather than spend an inordinate amount of time evaluating snowpit information from one spot. Some ways to help get the information you need are shown on the following pages.

Ski Pole/Hand Pit Test

This test takes only seconds and should be done often as you travel. Holding your ski pole at a right angle to the snow surface, gently push the handle end into the snowpack. In very soft snow, you can use the basket end of the pole. Obviously, boarders and snowmobilers will not have ski poles, but probes and even arms, ice axes, and shovel handles can be used to "feel" the snowpack in the same way. Feel the relative hardness and thickness of the layers. Is there an obvious softer, weak layer under a slab or does the snow feel homogenous? This is also a way to keep track of the depth and distribution of potential slabs. Probe in multiple spots, checking for variability in the layering.

Sometimes you may want to widen the hole with your pole (or arm) using circular motions. Reach into the hole and, with your fingers, feel how hard or soft each layer is. If you like, pull out some grains and examine their structure.

One serious limitation of the hand pit test is that sometimes the weak layers are too thin to detect by this method. Another is that it does not tell you how well the layers are actually bonded to each other, except in cases of extreme instability resulting from gross disconti- nuities. But it is fast and easy and if you get in the habit of poking and prodding the snowpack, you will be amazed at how much useful information you can glean.

Snowpit Tests (10-20 minutes)

Choose a spot with conditions similar to those you are trying to evaluate. In other words, select a site that has roughly the same elevation, snow conditions, and aspect as the slopes you are concerned about. Research has shown that stability tests do not have to be done on prime time slope angles. The advantage of picking test sites with angles around 25° is that it is easier to avoid or minimize your exposure to potential danger. The disadvantage for novices particularly, is that on lower angle slopes it can be more difficult to assess the shear quality and observe fractures within some kinds of test blocks (a good reason to get lots of practice digging pits and interpreting the results).

Often, you can dig at the top or along the edges of the slope you are interested in, but avoid obvious wind drifts just below a ridge crest where the snow depths are greater. Probe the area first to help locate a representative spot. If you detect areas where the snowpack is relatively thick and others where it is thin, you may want to check both, but pay special attention to the shallower areas. Fractures commonly initiate in thinner, weaker spots and then rip across into deeper, stronger snow. If there are several people in your group, have each person dig a quick pit in different places on the slope and then compare results. Balance safety with realism. Never conduct the following tests in a location where you might trigger a slide with serious consequences to yourself or others.

Generally, you should dig a pit 4-5 feet (1.25-1.5 m) deep and wide enough for you to work in (approximately 4 feet or 1.25 meters). Most human-triggered slab releases occur within this depth. If you are confident that you know where your weakest layer is, you only have to dig down to just below that layer. It is not usually necessary to dig to the ground unless that is where the weak layer of concern exists. However, it is a good idea to probe deeper than your pit—preferably all the way to the ground—to check for obvious weak layers. If you know that a storm just deposited more than 5 feet (1.5 m), especially if the new load came in on top of a sensitive layer like surface hoar, then dig deeper. The problem is that the deeper you dig, the more difficult it is to interpret your results. If you suspect deep slab instability, it is usually best to avoid the slope.

As you shovel, pay attention to changes in snow texture indicating weak and strong layers. Be careful not to disturb the snow surface surrounding the uphill portion of the pit. With your shovel, smooth off the uphill pit wall and adjacent, ideally shaded, side wall. These walls are where your tests will be conducted.

Identifying Layers:

The following procedures will help you determine whether or not you have a potentially unstable snow structure. Specifically, you are looking for a more cohesive slab layer overlying a less cohesive weak layer.

Stratigraphy Profile

Using a whisk broom, paint brush, hat, mitten, or a gloved hand, lightly brush the side wall of the pit with uniform strokes parallel to the snow surface. This will quickly transform the wall from a plain white surface into a layered mosaic of snow history. The layers

After brushing, strong and weak layers are quite evident in the wall of this snowpit.

73

of the snowpack will be revealed in a series of ridges and valleys.

The raised or ridged surfaces indicate the harder, stronger layers that may be possible slabs. The indentations or valleys reveal softer, weaker layers.

Resistance Profile

Using a portion of the sidewall that has not been brushed as described above, horizontally insert a rigid plastic or metal card, upside-down snow saw, or any straight edge approximately 2 inches (5 cm) into the top of the wall. Run the card down the wall, feeling the relative resistance of the layers and noting the boundaries of hard and soft layers. Pay particular attention to the location of weak layers that offer little resistance. Examining the layers in this way can help corroborate and expand upon the information gained from the stratigraphy profile.

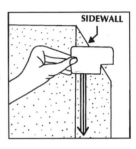

Hardness Profile

Test the relative hardness of each layer by gently pushing your hand or fingers into the pit wall, consistently applying about 2-3 pounds (1-1.5 kilograms) of pressure. One layer might be so soft that you can easily push your whole fist into it while another might require a knife to penetrate it. Layer hardness can be classified as fist (very soft), 4-finger (soft), 1-finger (medium), pencil (hard),

Very Soft	Fist (F)	
Soft	Four fingers (4F)	
Medium	One finger (1F)	
Hard	Pencil (P)	
Very Hard	Knife (K)	

Note: Test usually done with a gloved hand.

or knife (very hard). Alternatively, you can just run your thumbs or index fingers down the wall, pushing them in with equal force. This method is not as precise, but quickly yields the bottom line information.

An example of a potentially unstable configuration would be a cohesive 1-finger hard layer resting on top of a less cohesive, softer, fist hard layer. This, in turn, could be underlain by a harder bed (sliding) surface with a hardness ranging anywhere from 4-finger to knife. As discussed, however, the bed surface does not have to be hard. A slab over a well-developed weak layer will often feel like "something over nothing," but sometimes a potentially dangerous weak layer may be too thin to be detected by your hand or fingers.

Remember that the strength of a layer is determined by how well the grains within it are bonded to each other. While strong layers are often hard and weak layers are soft, note that this is not always the case. New powder snow can form cohesive slabs despite the fact that it might only be fist hard.

Testing Stability:

The profiling procedures just described yield a good visual representation of strong and weak layers, but still do not indicate how well the layers are bonded to each other and how much force it will take to make them fail. To check this, you must conduct snow stability tests. Such tests are critical because they may reveal a previously undetected but serious weakness in the snowpack created by poor bonding between layers or a very thin weak layer. Some of these tests can also give you information about whether or not cracks in the weak layer are likely to propagate.

To understand the results of the following stability tests, it is important to remember that stability is relative to the amount and rate of stress exerted on the snowpack. By applying increasing degrees of force, it is possible to gain a relative feel for the strength or bonding of the layers within the sample and relate this, along with other information, to the stability of the snowpack in a broader geographic area.

These tests require practice in the field to master. Their results can be misunderstood or misinterpreted, by experts as well as novices. We encourage you to experiment with these and other tests that have been developed and see which ones give you the best feel for snow stability.

Conduct these tests consistently, making sure that your blocks are the same size each time and that they are smooth and plumb (i.e., uniformly vertical). This will allow you to derive a meaningful scale and most reliably interpret your results. If your column is leaning or uneven, your test results will likely be biased (i.e., garbage in, garbage out).

Pay attention to the *ease* with which slab layers break and *how* they break as both are important indicators of how well the layers are bonded. The ease with which a column fails is rated as easy, moderate, or hard. Experience indicates the following: If the column fails while excavating or if you barely apply force and a layer shears off smooth, planar, and fast (i.e., almost jumps forward as if it is spring-loaded), the snowpack is unstable, with very poor layer bonding. Moderate fractures that are more difficult to initiate or sluggish in their response but break off cleanly may also indicate potentially unstable conditions (though they may be less easily triggered or require greater force to initiate release). Columns that have to be hammered loose or break on a rough, jagged, or uneven plane typically indicate a stable snowpack, provided that the test was conducted properly. The quality of the shear can be described using the scale below.

Description of Shear	Quality Rating
Breaks very easily and quickly along smooth, clean plane	Q1
Breaks on a smooth plane but more slowly and reluctantly	Q2
Breaks on a rough, jagged, or uneven plane	Q3

If in doubt about a particular test, retest to confirm your results. Keep in mind that a major limitation of any snowpit stability test is that we are measuring a small sample in one location and drawing conclusions about a much larger area. This is why integrating information from a wide variety of sources and locations is so critical. Also, if you get a test that is difficult to trigger, but it breaks very easily and quickly (Q1), be careful! You may have conditions where it is difficult to initiate a weak layer crack, but when you do the slope will fracture far and wide.

Compression Test (CT)

This is a relatively quick test involving a 12 inch by 12 inch (30 x 30 centimeter) isolated column of snow that will give you some idea of the force necessary to initiate a crack. Measure out a column and use a snow saw to isolate both sides. Then shovel back on one side of your column so that you can cut straight down behind the column with a snow saw. Be careful not to jar the column while cutting as this could bias your results. If you do not have a saw, isolate both sides of the column and cut the back by sawing vertically downward with a knotted cord. The column must be isolated on all sides. Now you are ready to apply increasing amounts of force on the column until you make it fail.

As seen on the left, the Compression Test starts with taps from the wrist. The CT test on the right produced an easy, Quality 1 shear on surface hoar. The shear plane is highlighted by the shovel. (Left photo by Bill Glude)

Place your shovel blade upside down on top of the column (so that it is horizontal and the shaft and handle are extending downhill into your pit). Tap vertically, applying the force straight down. The first ten taps should be articulated from your wrist and you should hit the shovel lightly with your fingertips. The next ten taps should be articulated from your elbow while you hit the shovel more forcefully with your flat hand. If the column still hasn't failed, hit the shovel with your fist, articulating the blows from your shoulder and letting the full weight of your arm drop.

Rating Compression Test Results	
Shear Failure	*Shear Rating*
1-10 taps (from wrist)	Easy
11-20 taps (from elbow)	Moderate
21-30 taps (from shoulder)	Hard

Extended Column Test (ECT)

In recent years, the Extended Column Test has become increasingly favored because it yields results that are relatively easy to interpret, gives information about both fracture initiation and propagation, and can be easily performed by all types of recreationists. This test is similar to the Compression Test except that the isolated column is larger. It should measure 3 feet (90 centimeters) across the slope and 12 inches (30 centimeters) up the slope. An effective way to isolate an ECT is to place a probe or ski pole vertically into the snow at each of the two uphill corners. Run a knotted string around the poles and pull it back and forth until you have cut deeper than the weak layer you are testing. This may take time if the snow is hard. You can also use a long saw or a saw mounted to a ski pole—just make sure to isolate the block without jarring it. A saw is also useful for smoothing the side walls of the column so that you are better able to observe your results. Now you are ready to apply force to one side of the column using the same steps as the Compression Test.

Blocks constructed as cleanly as for this ECT will yield the best results. (Photo by Amy O'Sadnick)

The ECT helps you determine not only how much force it will take to get the weak layer to fail, but also tests the propensity for a crack in the weak layer to propagate across the entire block. In general, weak layers that fracture across the entire block (known as ECTP) indicate unstable snow with a high probability of avalanching. By comparison, layers that do not fully propagate across the entire block (known as ECTN) are generally more stable and not as likely to avalanche. While the number and force of the taps reveals something about how easy or difficult it is to initiate a fracture, the key information provided by the ECT is whether or not the entire block fractures. All slopes producing a propagating ECT (ECTP) should be avoided or approached with caution by experienced travelers only after gathering considerable additional data.

Rutschblock Test (RB)

The Rutschblock Test allows you to test a larger area and gain a feeling for how sensitive the snowpack is to your weight. One disadvantage is that you have to move more snow so it may take more time unless you have several helpers in your group. Excavate the test site as indicated in the diagram, being careful not to disturb the area surrounding the shear block. Make sure the walls are even and plumb (vertical) before cutting the uphill wall with a snow saw, string, or ski. You are now ready. To save time, you can cut the sides of the block with a ski or snow saw rather than trenching. The drawback of this is that it can be more difficult to

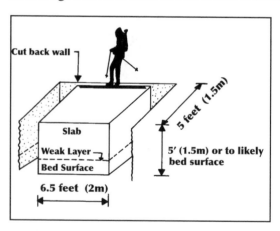

be sure you have completely isolated the rutschblock and therefore, test results may be flawed.

Note that the RB can be adapted by non-skiers. To do a rutschblock-like test, use the same principle of a standard block size to which successive degrees of force are applied. If you are a snowshoer or snowboarder, the block can be slightly narrower than the dimensions given, but trench uphill the same distance (5' or 1.5m) on either side before cutting the back. The same is true for snowmobilers and others who can just jump on foot though if you are dealing with very soft or thin slabs that are easy to break through, it is recommended that you make a "fanny landing."

The Rutschblock Test is good way to test the response of the snowpack to the weight of a person. This slab failed cleanly but sluggishly, and only after multiple jumps (RB6, Q2 on a 38° slope). What does this mean? What other tests or observations could confirm or refute this result? (Photo by Bill Glude)

Skiers performing a RB should carefully approach the block from above and step gently onto it. Once standing parallel and on the downhill side of the cut, flex your knees without lifting your heels in an attempt to apply light pressure to the shear block. Failure in either of these two steps indicates an unstable snowpack. If the slab doesn't fail, jump and land in the same compacted spot. Failure on this first jump also indicates instability. Gradually increase the force of your jumps. After repeated jumps, change your landing spot so that you are now landing almost mid-block. You might now remove your skis, particularly if you are dealing with a hard or deep slab, and jump several last times. Failure only after repeated jumps is a relatively strong test result. Again, remember that this does not prove the slope is stable, but it does give you greater confidence if the other bull's-eye clues are also pointing toward stability. Research has indicated that rutschblock scores may increase as slope angle decreases so be conservative and notch your score down a level if performing this test on less than prime time slope angles.

WHAT DO THE RUTSCHBLOCK TEST RESULTS MEAN?	
Level of Activity (Force)	**Degree of Instability**
1. Fails while excavating test site	Unstable
2. Fails while approaching or gently stepping onto block	Unstable
3. Fails while flexing knees	Unstable
4. Fails with one jump (with skis on)	Potentially unstable
5. Fails with two jumps (with skis on, same compacted spot)	Potentially unstable
6. Fails after repeated hard jumps (with or without skis)	Stable
7. Doesn't fail after repeated hard jumps (with skis off)	Stable or very stable

As with the Compression Test, it is important to observe the way the rutschblock fails. Pay more attention to failures that involve the entire block or most of the block, and that come off quickly and smoothly, like a rug being pulled out from underneath you. Failures that involve only part of the block may indicate less dangerous conditions but this is a fine line call and more data might be needed to make that determination.

"FALSE STABLE" TEST RESULTS

Research has shown that the snowpack on almost any given slope is highly variable, with strong and weak areas. Thus, a certain percentage of stability tests, even when dug in fairly representative locations by experienced observers, will provide "false stable" results. In other words, they will indicate stability when the slope is actually capable of avalanching. The "false stable" rate for the Rutschblock and Compression Tests is roughly 10% while it is about 5% for the Extended Column Test.

False stable results underscore the importance of using snowpit and stability test results to tell you that the snowpack in a given area is unstable but *not* to tell you it is stable unless these results are well corroborated by other bull's-eye data.

The surface hoar pictured has been redistributed by gentle winds. After the next storm, snowpits dug only a few feet apart could yield drastically different messages concerning snow stability. Build your stability evaluation by integrating data from multiple sources.

TESTING STABILITY BY TRYING TO TRIGGER AVALANCHES

One of the best ways to eliminate uncertainty about the stability of a given slope is to try to make it avalanche. Obviously, these tests are potentially hazardous and must be conducted from a safe location at the top of the slope, preferably by experienced travelers using bombproof belays. Make absolutely sure that there are no people, vehicles, buildings, or other fixed structures below you or on terrain adjacent to the slope you plan to trigger. This is critical in the increasingly crowded backcountry. If you are not 100% certain that the area is clear of people, do not proceed further. The best bet is to pick very small test slopes that do not feed into gullies or other terrain traps where you could be deeply buried. Select a short slope with a gentle runout. Even short cut banks or very small slopes (e.g. only 6-30 feet or 2-10m high) can yield extremely useful information about the instability in the area.

There are a number of ways to try to cause an avalanche. These include rolling large rocks or snow blocks onto the path from the ridge above (this is called trundling) or breaking off cornices (also known as the "bombs of the backcountry"). Cornices are very dangerous and should be approached with great caution. They can extend long distances laterally and it is common for them to snap off much further back than anticipated. Avoid large cornices, instead favoring small, fresh ones. Do not attempt to jump on a cornice, even with a good belay. Rather than putting the tester at risk, the best way to break off a section is to have two people standing on firm ground loop a knotted cord or climbing rope over the cornice and saw back and forth. Parachute cord or rope up to ¼ inch (5 millimeters) in diameter works best.

Another method is ski-testing, that is traversing slightly downslope across the top of a potential fracture zone, from safe spot to safe spot while applying force into the snowpack. Be advised that this test can kill you and should be done only on small slopes by expert skiers or snowboarders, with a spotter watching, and only if the instability involves soft surface layers (as opposed to hard or deep slab instability). Do not attempt to ski cut large slopes. Make sure you are using releasable bindings. Remember that such a ski test does not at all ensure that the slope is now safe to ski. Snow conditions can vary greatly from the top to the bottom of a slope.

Many people have ski tested the upper part of a slope, assumed it was safe, and then triggered an avalanche while descending.

Recognize that even if you do not succeed in triggering an avalanche, the slope is not necessarily stable and may still avalanche when you attempt to travel on it. Maybe you did not apply enough force or affect the most sensitive trigger zone. A slope that may be safe for the first two travelers might release when a third person enters the slope. As with snowpits, do not rely solely on these tests to decide that the slope is stable.

Jumping on this short, steep slope provided instant bull's-eye feedback. Choose low consequence, small test slopes and if you suspect instability, don't let your guard down if you can't get the snow to release. As the saying goes, if you smell a skunk, it is probably hidden close by, even if you can't see it and others are pretending it is not there.

GATHERING EVIDENCE FROM RECENT AVALANCHES:

When we dig snowpits and conduct shear tests, we are trying to surmise what kind of layering exists and how sensitive any weak layers are to force. There is a fair amount of conjecture involved and, of course, the information is only reliable for evaluating snow stability if we have successfully chosen a representative location.

One of the best ways to learn about the instability that might be lurking in the snowpack and for that matter, about avalanches in general, is to examine recently released avalanches. Do not miss the opportunity, provided you can do so safely (i.e., the fracture line has broken near the ridge, there is no "hangfire" or threat from nearby slopes, there are no hazards such as a cliff below, and you have safe access to the site). The "crime" has already been committed and you are now the detective on scene.

To conduct a fracture profile, use your shovel and cut a short distance back from the fracture line so that you have a clean, fresh vertical wall. Identify the layers using the same methods as for a snowpit. Keep in mind that the weakest snow has already slid. So if you cannot detect a weak layer or discontinuity at the fracture line, move over to the flanks or just beyond them. What is the depth, distribution, and hardness of the slab? How did the weather influence slab formation? What is the weak layer? Again, take note of the hardness and thickness. When was the weak layer likely to have formed and under what conditions? What triggered the slide? Can you identify any likely trigger zones?

Measure the bed surface slope angle and try to determine how the terrain influenced how and where the slide broke. Often, the slope above the fracture line is several degrees less than the bed surface slope angle. Use your inclinometer to measure the runout angle, that is, the angle between the fracture line and the farthest extent of the slide (i.e., the toe of the debris or end of the powderblast zone). This angle (which must not be confused with slope angle) is an indication of the runout efficiency of a given avalanche. The lower the angle, the more efficient and longer-running the slide. Very long-running slides may have runout angles in the mid-high teens or low 20's while avalanches that run only a short distance might have runout angles in the 30's. These angles will vary by regional snow climate and with individual storms. Knowing the runout angles of avalanches that are releasing will help you determine how far away you need to stay from steep slopes that could potentially avalanche. Whenever you are establishing safe spots to stop or setting up a camp and wondering if you are clear of potential danger, you can measure a runout angle from where you are standing to where you think the slope could fracture. The lower the angle, the safer you are.

If the avalanche is recent, it may help you greatly reduce your uncertainty about current conditions. Older fracture lines will not provide reliable information about the current stability or even necessarily the layering that existed at the time of the avalanche. In any case, if you make a habit of studying the evidence left behind by avalanches, asking questions, and piecing together the contributory factors, you will be much better able to anticipate when, where, and how avalanches are likely to occur.

The runout angle of this avalanche, measured from the fracture line to the toe of the debris, was 22.5°. This was a relatively efficient, long-running avalanche given the vertical drop of the path, but under exceptional conditions the avalanche could run even further. If the debris had stopped further upslope, the angle would have been higher, indicating a less efficient slide.

What are Your Alternatives & Their Possible Consequences?

Thus far, we have discussed the physical factors—the terrain, snow-pack, and weather variables—that make it possible for a slope to avalanche. But if you are reading *Snow Sense* because you want to avoid dying or killing others in an avalanche, then read this section very, very carefully.

It is possible to travel at times of high snow instability by choosing safe routes (if they exist). Similarly, we can get caught in an avalanche during periods of relatively low snow instability through poor stability evaluation and route selection. In other words, we create potential hazard by traveling in avalanche terrain and we can control the degree of hazard we face on most days given good decision-making.

The terms hazard and risk are often used interchangeably, but they are not the same. *Hazard* takes into account the physical attributes of the exposure to potential danger—for example, the intensity of the storm or the slope steepness. *Risk* is the chance of something going wrong—the hazard multiplied by the consequences. It is a personal choice, the "what's going to happen to me" part of the equation.

We live in a society that tends to glorify risk, blithely airbrushing away the potential consequences. We laud risk when it succeeds and denigrate it as reckless when it does not. By definition, some risky ventures are going to fail. Managing risk is a balancing act between a desired outcome and the probability of achieving it. Knowing your goal is key because it is your "yardstick for success" and helps determine how much you are willing to put at risk.

If your objective is to climb a new, very exposed route, all members of your group must be willing to accept a higher level of risk than a group heading outside to enjoy a beautiful day. Just make sure that the risk is truly understood by all. Commonly, travelers are willing to assume high levels of risk until someone gets injured or killed, and then their actions no longer seem worth the consequences. A greater challenge than taking risks can be learning to minimize them—it can be harder to be cautious than to be bold.

People with high risk-taking attitudes generally filter information about potential hazard and draw unrealistically optimistic conclusions that lead them to push the fine line even finer. When pushing close to this edge, there is less room for error and it takes smaller mistakes to get into trouble. People who are generally conservative by nature look at the same information, but with a different filter that allows them to further justify their conservative approach. In examining accidents, we have found it fascinating that travelers with different attitudes toward risk have used exactly the same data to draw completely opposite conclusions.

Most of us don't feel like we are negotiating hazard and making decisions with bags over our heads but the truth is that we are routinely blinded by our needs, our desires, the pressures being exerted on us, and by our previous experience. (Photo from Blaine Smith collection)

Most of those who have died in avalanches knew better. They had either been explicitly warned of the hazard or had enough knowledge to recognize the key clues. How could some have looked at clear evidence of danger and not "seen" it? How could still others have seen the signs and chosen to ignore them, overestimating their ability to deal with the hazard? We do not have to look far for the answer. All of us do this to some extent every day. After every accident, we seem to feel the need to quickly assign blame, if only because it makes us feel less vulnerable. Before you are too quick to label the victims "stupid," bear in mind that we are all subject to the same pitfalls of human perception. When we permit ourselves to be blinded by one or more of the following "human factors," we allow avalanche accidents to happen.

HUMAN FACTORS THAT COMMONLY CAUSE AVALANCHE ACCIDENTS	
• ATTITUDE	• INDECISION
• EGO	• HASTE
• POOR PLANNING	• COMPLACENCY
• DENIAL	• SUMMIT FEVER
• TUNNEL VISION	• MONEY CONSIDERATIONS
• OVERCONFIDENCE	• LAZINESS
• PEER PRESSURE	• FATIGUE
• POOR COMMUNICATION	• INATTENTION

A CLOSER LOOK AT HUMAN FACTORS

Attitude is one of the main causes of avalanche accidents as it leads us to filter data and warp it to our needs and desires. The more we want to do something—whether it is to get married or jump onto a particular slope—the more likely we are to make assumptions that go unchecked and to pay attention only to the data that tells us what we want to hear. In that sense, we are like the Texas sharpshooter who plugs the side of a barn and then draws bull's-eyes around the bullet holes.

You are undoubtedly familiar with this logo, but have you ever noticed the arrow between the E and the x? Alas, you will now see it every time a FedEx truck drives by... We assume that if we just keep our eyes open, we will see whatever there is to be seen. The reality, however, is that we tend to see what we expect to see, what we want to see, or what we have seen before. Though he had spent a lifetime in the mountains, the brother of a snowmobiler killed in an avalanche says, "I'd seen three avalanches before my brother's accident. Now I've seen thousands. I'll be driving and I'll see one ripped out to dirt four miles off the road. I see them everywhere I go."

Avalanches are not concerned about our beliefs, schedules, or goals. It does not matter to an unstable slope that our ego is at stake, that we're suffering from tunnel vision, or that we are fatigued and cold. It is irrelevant that we are emboldened by sunshine or cameras, that we're being subjected to peer pressure, that we're afraid to look cowardly, that darkness is approaching, or that we have to be back at work on Monday. It makes no difference that we excel at our sport or feel comfortable with the slope because we have played on it for years.

Other human factors that repeatedly get us into trouble include the "sheep syndrome" (blindly following whoever is leading; also known as the herding instinct), the "cow syndrome" (a rush to get back to the barn at the end of the day), and the "lion syndrome" (a rush for first tracks or ephemeral powder). And while we often feel safer in herds, the reality is that big groups actually decrease our safety because it is difficult to communicate, make objective decisions, and follow safe travel procedures. The bigger the group, the more emboldened we are likely to be.

ASSUMPTIONS

Human factors are often rooted in the assumptions we make. Here are examples of assumptions that have resulted in avalanche fatalities.

"The forecast center said the hazard was moderate so we didn't expect to get caught." Note: Make your own stability evaluations. Hazard forecasts are regional, not site-specific. They are starting points in your decision-making process, but are not *the* answer. Accidents often happen on moderate hazard days when the instability is localized rather than widespread.

"We thought it was safe because there were already tracks on the slope." Note: Tracks might make us *feel* safer, but they do not mean that the slope is safe. Maybe no one has hit the tender spot on the slope or not quite enough stress has yet been exerted.

"I'd ridden to that place dozens of times and never seen an avalanche." Note: The snowpack is usually stable so we relax our guard and begin to think of an area as safe. If the site is avalanche terrain, it will eventually produce avalanches. Ten years is a long period of observation with respect to a human life but it is nothing more than a wink in the life of an avalanche path. If we allow experience to let us become complacent, it can be as much a blindfold as it is a guide.

"October seemed way too early for avalanches—there was only 9 inches (23 centimeters) of snow." Note: Avalanches can hap-

pen in any month that there is snow on the ground (even if only an inch or two). Integrate other key pieces of data including the roughness of the ground surface and slope angle.

"With blue sky, perfect powder, and no sign of avalanches, it just seemed like a day where nothing could go wrong." Note: Denial is a common human trait and one that is hard to fight, especially when we feel invincible on a gorgeous day and might not be allowing ourselves to see the clues. Also understand that every avalanche cycle must have its first avalanche event. While most natural avalanches happen during new snow and wind-loading events, the majority of human-triggered avalanches occur on the nice days after storms. This is because: 1) most people do not travel in white-out conditions, and 2) the new load has increased the stress on the snowpack and may or may not have caused natural releases, depending upon the strength of the snowpack. When we go outside hungry for new powder, we may be all that is needed to trigger the slope.

"We were wearing rescue beacons so we figured we would be OK even if we got caught." Note: A functioning beacon just means that the beacon will be recovered. Too many times, people wearing beacons have died from mechanical injuries during the ride, suffocated before they were dug out, and/or not been found quickly because the other members of the party were also caught or did not know how to search effectively. If you find yourself feeling reassured by your beacon or any other avalanche safety device, the real message is that you are in the wrong place at the wrong time and you need to take an alternative course of action.

We planned the trip for six months and weren't about to throw it all away because of one storm. Besides, it was our third try at climbing this mountain." Note: Timing is everything.

THE "SO WHAT?" TEST

As a filter for the human factors that bias objectivity, get in the habit of subjecting the rationale behind your decisions to the "so what?" test. The catch is that you must answer from the mountain's perspective. So what, does the mountain care that you've been working overtime for weeks and are desperate to test out your new gear? Not at all. So what, does the mountain care that more than 3 feet (1 meter) of snow fell overnight after a week of cold, clear weather? Absolutely—a fair amount of load was deposited in a short amount of time, likely burying weak layers of surface hoar and/or near-surface facets. Whenever you are on or near steep, snow-covered slopes, regardless of slope size or time of year, you need to think like an avalanche.

Think about the potential consequences of your actions. What assumptions are you making? What are your chances of success versus your chances of getting caught, buried, or killed? Is it worth it? Do better alternatives exist?

As far as the snowpack is concerned, a bomb is about to land on this 50° slope. It's too late to ask if you've assessed conditions carefully or chosen the right timing. The bottom line question is what's going to happen if you get caught? (Photo taken by Bill Glude in the Coast Mountains, southeast Alaska during very stable weather and snow conditions).

Decision-Making: Using the Avalanche Hazard Evaluation Checklist

Skilled avalanche hazard evaluation is based upon a systematic decision-making process in which you:

❋ Identify potential problems.

❋ Continuously collect, evaluate, and integrate ◎ data (i.e, facts, observations, and test results that have a high degree of certainty in their message).

❋ Explore your alternatives and their possible consequences.

❋ Make a decision followed by action.

❋ Re-evaluate your decision if necessary based upon new information or changing conditions.

Sound decision-making demands good communication between group members. Exchange information and suggestions freely. Evaluate each other's assumptions. Keep in mind that not having a clear plan or making an explicit decision is a decision by default.

Never be reluctant to say, "NO, I don't think that is a good route because…" Equally important, learn to accept a "no" from another group member. A "no" based upon facts is a very powerful tool with which to save lives.

Decades ago, when we first became involved with avalanche rescue and accident investigations, it struck us that most groups had some inkling of the potential instability *before* the avalanche occurred. It seemed to us that if we could design a checklist, similar to those routinely used by even experienced pilots during take-offs and landings, maybe it would be easier for backcountry travelers to organize and recognize the significance of key pieces of information. The resulting *avalanche hazard evaluation checklist* is a summary of the bottom line questions that need to be asked and answered when evaluating avalanche hazard. Imprint it onto your brain and use it as a framework for making your decisions.

But as use of the checklist became more widespread, we noticed another disturbing trend. Survivors would use the checklist to tell us exactly why the accident had happened. For example, we were commonly told, "We knew it was steep and wind-loaded and we heard some whumphing noises, but…" There always seemed to be a "but." So in an attempt to make it more difficult to rationalize or overlook the message, we adopted the idea of traffic lights. Get in the habit of always designating each critical piece of data as a red, yellow, or green light.

Red lights: Danger, a hazardous situation exists.

Yellow lights: Be cautious, there is potential hazard, too much uncertainty, or conditions are deteriorating.

Green lights: It's OK, no hazard exists.

For example, slopes that are less than 25° and are not connected to anything steeper can be given a green light. Remember that you can be standing on the flats but are in red light terrain if there is a steeper slope adjacent to you. Slopes that have no components steeper than 25°-30° and are not connected to steeper slopes can be considered yellow lights under most conditions. They are capable of producing avalanches but relatively infrequently and during periods of fairly obvious instability. During questionable or highly unstable conditions, these slopes should be considered red lights. Slopes above 30° are more likely to produce avalanches under a wider range of conditions and thus are red lights. The potential hazard rises quickly and the red light gets much brighter as slope angles increase to the mid-30's and above. A 36° slope is unequivocally a red light. Automatically, the overall light for terrain will be red unless there are extenuating circumstances (e.g., the slope is windward and completely stripped of snow or so thickly forested that it is very difficult to even travel through the trees).

The effects of past weather will be reflected in snowpack conditions. So when you are assigning lights to the primary weather variables (precipitation, wind, and temperature), you are evaluating whether current conditions are likely to make the snow more unstable. The amount and rate of change are obviously of critical importance.

Indications of a green light snowpack include lack of clues indicating instability (e.g., no shooting cracks or whumphing noises, recent avalanche activity, hollow sounds, etc) and hard, low quality (Q3) stability test results.

It is relatively easy to assign green or red lights to critical factors when the snow is obviously stable or very unstable. It is far more difficult when the instability is moderate and the problem areas are less widespread. Under these conditions, you might be in the mountains all day, seeing few or no clues to instability and getting medium test results. Natural avalanches might not be occurring though there is lingering potential for human-triggered releases on selected angles and aspects.

If you are getting yellow lights, evaluate whether they are due to uncertainty, variability in conditions, or because conditions are changing for the worse. If uncertainty is the problem, see if you can gather more data to turn the light into a definite red or green. If conditions are changing, monitor the rate of change. Under yellow light conditions, it is more imperative than ever to stay vigilant, keep evaluating, and be conservative. You might not find a trouble spot until the end of the day.

When the critical data is integrated, a more complete message starts to appear. For example, you might be on 38° prime time red light terrain, but if all the critical snowpack and weather factors are green lights, from the point of view of an avalanche, you have a green light to go do whatever you choose on that slope. **Make a habit of using the checklist, assigning lights, and staying open to the message.**

AVALANCHE HAZARD EVALUATION CHECKLIST

Critical Data		Hazard Rating*		
PARAMETERS:	**KEY INFORMATION**	**G**	**Y**	**R**

TERRAIN: *Is the terrain capable of producing an avalanche?*

	G	Y	R
• Slope angle (steep enough to slide? prime time?)	○	○	○
• Slope aspect (leeward, shadowed, or very sunny?)	○	○	○
• Slope configuration (anchoring? terrain trap?)	○	○	○
Overall Terrain Rating:	○	○	○

WEATHER: *Is the weather contributing to instability?*

	G	Y	R
• Precipitation (type? amount and intensity of load?)	○	○	○
• Wind (loading? where, how much, how fast?)	○	○	○
• Temperature (storm trends? effects of warming/cooling?)	○	○	○
Overall Weather Rating:	○	○	○

SNOWPACK: *Could the snow slide?*

	G	Y	R
• Unstable snow structure (depth & distribution?)	○	○	○
• Bonding (weak layer? trigger zones?)	○	○	○
• Force (how easy to trigger? stability tests? clues?)	○	○	○
Overall Snowpack Rating:	○	○	○

HUMAN: *What are your alternatives and their possible consequences?*

	G	Y	R
• Attitude (toward risk? goal? assumptions?)	○	○	○
• Blinders (denial? peer pressure? group size/communication?)	○	○	○
• Decision-making (avalanche skills? level of uncertainty?)	○	○	○
Overall Human Rating:	○	○	○

DECISION/ ACTION:

Overall Hazard Rating   *GO* ○ *or NO GO* ○

* HAZARD LEVEL SYMBOLS: R= Red light (stop/dangerous), G = Green light (go/okay), Y = Yellow light (caution/potentially dangerous).

LOOKING AT DATA OBJECTIVELY

Let's look at various combinations of red, green, and yellow lights in terms of the bottom line—can we go (green light) or not (red light)?

Data		TERRAIN	WEATHER	SNOWPACK	HUMAN	GO/NO GO
	1.	R	R	R	G	R
	2.	G	G	G	G	G
	3.	R	G	R	G	R
Scenario #	4.	R	G	G	G	G
	5.	R	R	G	G	G/Y→R
	6.	G	R	R	G	G
	7.	R	Y	Y	G	R
Key: R=Red light, G=Green light, Y=Yellow light						

Notice that in all of the scenarios, we have assigned a green light to the human factor although, in reality, it is usually a yellow or a red and a major contributing factor to accidents. Your perfect group is limited in size to three people who are open-minded and communicate well, are well trained (i.e., have good avalanche hazard evaluation, travel procedure, and rescue skills) and well equipped. The goal of the group is to have fun in great snow and go home at the end of the day.

With the terrain, weather, and snowpack in scenario #1 all red lights, the answer to the question "go or no go?" is obviously a "no go" or red light. Similarly, if terrain, weather, and snowpack are all green lights (scenario #2), you can safely travel the slope.

Now, as shown in scenario #3, suppose the terrain is red (e.g., 35°, leeward), the weather is green (e.g., blue sky, calm, no temperature changes contributing to instability), and the snowpack is red (e.g., 14 inches or 36 centimeters of new and wind-deposited snow, poorly bonded to the old snow surface). Do you go or not? The answer is a resounding red light signaling STOP! Note that while this seems obvious, the majority of accidents occur during these nice weather conditions. **Regardless of the weather, anytime the terrain and snowpack are red lights, it is a no go situation.**

Scenario #4 with red terrain, green weather, and green snowpack is a dream day for many recreationists. You can climb a couloir, or highmark a 40° slope, or ski/snowboard the steep stuff.

Scenario #5 with red terrain, red weather, and a green snowpack is more marginal. You need to evaluate how fast conditions are deteriorating and how long you will be exposed to potential danger. This is one of the few situations in which party strength and travel abilities could make a difference. Strong groups may be able to safely go quickly while for weaker, slower parties, it is certainly a yellow light and, even more likely, a red light situation.

Let's say from a recreationist's point of view that it has been a terrible winter, with very little snow. From an avalanche perspective, thin snow cover often means a weak snowpack of faceted grains. Now, finally a big storm has rolled in. You are desperate to get outside. The snowpack is trying to adjust to the increased stress that is being exerted upon it. This is where your attitude could get you into trouble. Take yourself to a place where you have a choice of slope angles. If you find that the snowpack is a red, you simply have to notch the terrain back to a green. This is the situation shown in Scenario #6 with green terrain, red weather, and a red snowpack. You can have a great day playing on slopes with angles in the low 20's where there is high instability but no hazard because these slopes—and the ones they are connected to—are not steep enough to slide. Just make sure that you do not stumble onto red terrain, which can happen quickly, particularly in poor visibility, when traversing, or when dropping over convexities.

In Scenario #7, with red terrain and yellow light weather and snowpack, it is safest to consider it a red light or "no go" situation. **When in doubt or when conditions are changing rapidly, be conservative in your hazard evaluation and route selection decisions, leaving a margin for error. The greater your uncertainty or the greater the consequences of an error in your judgment, the wider the margin needs to be.**

"We never thought it was steep enough to slide. It couldn't have been more than 10° where we were though it was really steep up higher. Then suddenly, the entire slope broke loose and came down on us. We had heard some whumphing noises earlier, but didn't pay much attention. The storm ended yesterday and the weather today was bluebird." Anonymous survivor. Interpretation: Terrain=Red, Snowpack=Red, Weather=Green. Most accidents occur under these conditions.

Remember that the purpose of seeking information is to reduce or eliminate uncertainty about conditions. The mountain environment isn't static and potential hazard can, and often does, change within a few minutes or literally, a few feet. Keep evaluating every step of the way.

Traveling Smart: Route Selection and Safe Travel Principles

Careful route selection can greatly reduce your chances of getting caught in an avalanche and, in some areas, make it possible for you to travel during periods of high instability. When in the mountains, you can't necessarily travel in a straight line. Sometimes whether you go a few feet to the right or left can make all the difference with respect to your safety. The tenets of safe route selection are based upon the following three concepts:

❄ Prepare for the worst.

❄ Use the terrain to your advantage.

❄ Minimize your exposure time and use safe travel procedures.

PREPARE FOR THE WORST

Familiarize yourself with the terrain, preferably even before going into the field. For example, if planning a climb, use aerial and oblique photographs, maps, and local knowledge to identify potentially hazardous or crux areas as well as safety zones. During your approach, view the route from as many perspectives as possible. Identify your alternatives.

Check current conditions as well as weather and avalanche forecasts before you leave. Take note of the expected precipitation (i.e., types, amounts, storm duration), freezing level, wind speed and direction, and temperature trends. Do not just hone onto the forecasted avalanche danger levels but pay attention to the specific information given concerning potential problem areas and weak layers. Don't let your guard down if the forecasted avalanche danger is low or moderate. Try to get site-specific, real-time observations from those who have recently been in the area.

Know the capabilities of your group. Are your partners capable of doing the trip or tackling the slope you have in mind? Do not be forced into splitting your group—this has led to a large number of accidents. Don't be afraid of reconsidering your plan. Establish and agree upon the purpose of your trip (e.g., have fun, reach the summit no matter what, etc.). Keep your groups small. Groups larger than 4-6 people tend to feel invincible and often have a difficult time making decisions quickly, communicating, keeping track of each other, and following safe travel procedures.

Prepare for emergencies. Necessary equipment includes a functioning brain, inclinometer, avalanche rescue equipment (shovel, beacon, and probe at a minimum), and survival/first aid gear. You may choose to file a trip plan with a responsible person before leaving. If so, leave a reasonable amount of time for bad weather. Trip plans can trap parties into poor decision-making and trying, against the odds, to return by the "deadline." Fear that a search will be launched is not justification for exposing a group to risk.

USE THE TERRAIN TO YOUR ADVANTAGE

For example, favor the windward sides of ridges, avoid lee slopes until you have had the chance to check them out, or stay well out in the valley bottoms away from avalanche-producing slopes. Measuring slope angles will help you determine the safest route. When in doubt, take the known over the unknown.

You can become an avalanche victim by:

❋ Ignoring slight but significant increases in slope angle (this is very easy to do when traversing or dropping over a convexity);

❋ Traveling with steep slopes above and/or hazardous terrain traps such as cliffs, ravines, and creek bottoms below (think consequences);

❋ Forgetting that it is possible to trigger an avalanche from a low angle slope or a ridge as long as where you are standing is connected to avalanche terrain and sensitive instability exists;

❋ Overlooking subtle changes in snow conditions caused by wind or sun due to variations in slope aspect;

❋ Presuming that a summer trail or road is necessarily a safe winter route;

❋ Crossing a slope at or below a high stress point such as a convex rollover;

❋ Assuming tree-covered slopes are safe (remember, if you can travel through the trees, an avalanche can run through them);

❋ Traveling on top of or underneath cornices, particularly those that have been recently loaded or warmed (do not forget about cornice crevasses); and;

❋ Traveling on a slope that has not yet slid as opposed to using the nearby bed surface of a recent avalanche. If the slope has fractured near ridge level and has not re-loaded, the bed surface can be a very safe route up, down, or across.

Whether a given route is "good" or "bad" depends largely on the stability of the snow as well as the consequences of getting caught. The route pictured is potentially dangerous — the slope has an angle of 38°, it is poorly anchored, leeward, and there is evidence of vegetative damage from previous avalanches. If the slope fractures, you may have difficulty escaping to the edge and may get slammed against the trees. Under stable conditions, this route is perfectly acceptable.

MINIMIZE YOUR EXPOSURE TIME AND USE SAFE TRAVEL PROCEDURES

Safe travel procedures include exposing one person at a time to potential hazard while all other members of the party watch the exposed person from safe spots. This not only minimizes the number of people who will get caught if something goes wrong, thus maximizing your available rescue resources, but also reduces the stress being exerted upon the snowpack.

❄ **Do not travel above your partner.**

❄ **Do not travel out of sight of each other.**

❄ **Do not stop in the middle of or at the bottom of steep slopes.**

Don't just follow these safe travel procedures when you think you might need them. Make them a habit you never break and they might just save you if you make an error in judgment. Minimize the amount of time you are exposed to hazard by knowing your route, traveling as quickly as possible, and being skilled in your method of travel. Turn back to page 105 and read this message over—it could save your life.

Snowboarder and skier accidents have happened when one person stopped to take a picture of the other descending toward him. If you have to stop, do so at the edge of a slope (beyond the flanks of the slab), where you have some protection from the terrain or vegetation, or well beyond the runout zone of the path. Many snowmobiler fatalities have occurred when one rider stopped or became stuck on a steep slope and a partner rode or highmarked above him.

Always think about potential escape routes—have in mind your quickest exit from hazard because you will only have a split second to react. If using ski poles, do not wear the straps around your wrist and ski or snowboard with releasable bindings, preferably with no safety straps (brakes are fine). If you are caught in an avalanche and cannot shed your equipment, it can act like an anchor and drag you down into the flowing debris.

If ascending: Favor gentle angles and the margins of slopes. Avoid long traverses with steep slopes above you. When possible, use ridge routes but remember that ridges can produce avalanches if the terrain is steep enough and beware of cornices. If you are on skis ascending a narrow ridge, you need to make your zigzags similarly narrow even though it might mean a lot of kick turns. Sometimes, climbing straight up on foot may be your safest, fastest line but this depends greatly on the snowpack as floundering in the snow or kicking steps can put a lot of stress on the snowpack.

If crossing: Where possible, minimize your exposure by cross-ing on gentler slope angles or well out into the runout zone. If the slope is uniformly steep, you might want to cross as high as possible (if there are no terrain traps below), above the likely frac-ture zone, or at least where any moving snow has little chance of gaining momentum before it reaches you. If using cliff bands for protection, stay high, almost on the rocks where the snow may be more compacted and stronger due to previous sluffing off of the cliff faces. Remember also that there may be stress concentration areas a short distance below the rocks where the snow is able to flow downslope more freely. If the slope is too wide to keep your partners in sight, maintain visual contact by traveling one at a time from safe spot to safe spot. Make sure the safe spots are really protected (e.g., a windswept ridge or anchors that you can grab without being swept away by moving snow from above). If possible, cross the slope at a slight downhill traverse to minimize your exposure time. Sometimes, using the same traverse track will minimize disturbance to the snow as well as exposure time, but this depends on the given snowpack. If you are nervous about cross-ing or there are no safe spots, find an alternate route or consider trying to trigger the slope before crossing.

If descending: If you want to travel on steep slopes, approach them from above whenever possible. Start by descending slopes with gentler angles and then if you get confirmation of your stabil-ity evaluation, you can work your way onto steeper terrain. It is often a good idea to favor the sides of a slope rather than the middle so that you have a better chance of escaping off to the edge of a slab. Choose slopes where you can see the entire run and that have gradual, open runout zones rather than cliffs, gullies, or dense trees below. Be suspicious of steep rollovers or other potential trigger zones such as rocky or thin snowpack areas. Wherever you can, take advantage of natural protection such as ridges (though keep in mind that fractures can wrap over and around some ridges and stay off of cornices) or the bed surface and/or debris edge of previous slides.

(continued on page 110)

Sledding Smart in Avalanche Country

ATTENTION SNOWMOBILERS: If you want to cut the annual number of snowmobiler fatalities by more than 50%:

ALLOW ONLY ONE RIDER AT A TIME ON AVALANCHE SLOPES <u>AND</u> DO NOT PARK AT THE BOTTOM.

Here are some other major ways to maximize the safety of your group:

❄ **Carefully watch your partner from a safe spot.** To improve your chances in case you have misjudged the terrain, park your sled pointing downhill or facing the quickest avenue of escape, keep the sleds parallel so they don't block each other, and have the kill switch up or the sled running.

The rider who parked here died under four feet of avalanche debris.

❄ **If a person gets stuck, do not send a second rider to help.** Many of the snowmobiler avalanche fatalities have occurred when two riders are tugging on a sled (more than 1000 pounds/450 kilos on one spot in the snow) or when a second rider turns above the stuck person and triggers a slab onto his partner.

❄ **Rescue equipment should be on the rider, not attached to the sled or under the hood.** Strap your beacon to your chest and wear a small pack with a probe and shovel.

If You Highmark: Recognize that highmarking is risky because you are approaching steep slopes from the bottom with millions of pounds of snow hanging above you. Highmarking accounts for more than 60% of the avalanche deaths involving snowmobilers in North America. It is not unusual for multiple snowmobilers to track up a slope before it rips out so do not be reassured just because there are already tracks. The following strategies will help increase your chances of success.

❋ **Pick the right timing.** There are days to highmark steep terrain and days to avoid it like the plague. Recent avalanche activity is Mother Nature's #1 sign that instability exists.

❋ **Be very wary of recently wind-loaded slopes.** Remember that snow that is rock hard can still avalanche if it is poorly bonded to the layers before.

❋ **Select slopes that have recently avalanched (and not reloaded significantly) over those with similar aspects that have not yet slid.** If you are unsure of the snow stability, just choose slopes less than 25° that are not connected to anything steeper.

❋ **Avoid terrain traps such as gullies, concave bowls, or steep-sided creek bottoms because of the high probability of a deep burial.** In traps where all the debris piles up in the depression, it is not uncommon for riders to be buried under 10-30 feet (3-10 meters) of debris.

❋ **Favor slopes that are fan-shaped** (this may help the debris spread out). **Try to avoid slopes with serious hazards like cliffs, boulders, or dense trees below.**

❋ **Test ride small slopes before committing to bigger ones. Ride the edges of a slope rather than "center-punching" it.** Do your first runs low and fast instead of maximizing your commitment and exposure by climbing as high as possible right away. If you can, do your first runs from the top down to get a feel for the snow and improve your chances of escape.

(continued from page 107)

If you are going to fall, try to sit gently rather than crash in order to minimize the force of the "bomb" (stress) you put into the slope. For the same reason, do not land jumps on a slope unless you are very sure of the stability. However, if you are thinking that a slope is safe *unless* you land a hard jump, fall, or get your sled stuck, then you are cutting the line too fine and should pick a different slope. Decide which descent line the group will use on a given run. Make sure only one person descends the slope at a time while all others watch. Establish a safe stopping point. Have prearranged signals so that you are sure the exposed person is clear before the next person starts to descend. Just in case, keep track of the closest, best escape route.

Know that sometimes there may be no safe route. If, however, you have instability on a route that absolutely must be descended, you may have the option of turning your worst enemy into your best friend by triggering an avalanche and then descending the slide path. This is far better than taking your chances and springing a waiting trap. Continually reassess your alternatives—often better choices exist even if you don't recognize them right away.

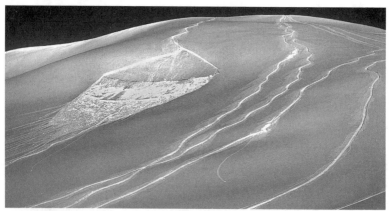

Sometimes, depending on the instability, a variation of only a few degrees in slope angle makes the difference between triggering a slide and avoiding the problem all together. The bed surface of this skier-triggered slab was 38° while the slope to the right was 35°. (Photo from Chuck O'Leary collection, AMSC)

Avalanche Rescue

The best strategy is to avoid getting caught because avalanche rescue does not work very well. Asphyxiation is the primary killer of avalanche victims, accounting for roughly 75% of all fatalities. Statistically, one out of every three people who are completely buried in an avalanche will die. Approximately 25% of avalanche victims die from trauma (primarily head injuries—wear a helmet). If you travel alone or without essential safety equipment and/or have not formulated and practiced a rescue plan, you are greatly limiting your chances of survival if caught in an avalanche. **You do not have time to go for help. YOU ARE THE HELP.**

Essential equipment for *each* member of a group to carry <u>and</u> know how to use includes:

* ❄ Avalanche rescue transceiver (beacon)

* ❄ Avalanche probe

* ❄ Shovel

You might also consider wearing an Avalung™ and/or an avalanche airbag. Developed relatively recently, these devices have saved lives and are becoming increasingly popular. One caution about all avalanche safety equipment: if you let your gear make you feel safer, you are more likely to act in less safe ways that increase the chances of getting into trouble.

An *avalanche rescue transceiver or beacon* is a small electronic device capable of transmitting and receiving a signal within a range of approximately 100 to 200+ feet (30-60+ meters). All beacons on the market use a standardized frequency (457 kHz) and are compatible with each other. For the duration of a trip, each member of the group wears a transmitting beacon strapped to his or her chest (and protected inside clothing). Should an avalanche bury someone, all survivors switch their beacons to receive mode, spread out across the debris, and begin the search using a pattern recommended by the manufacturer (and hopefully practiced assiduously before venturing into avalanche terrain). Once a signal is picked up, the location of the buried beacon can usually be pinpointed within 2-4 minutes by a skilled searcher.

Beacons are a reliable means of finding a completely buried person but offer no defense against trauma, suffocation, and hypothermia. While they have increased the survival rate, still roughly half of those armed with beacons are dug out dead. Beacons will not help you if you use poor travel procedures and all members of your party are buried. And you cannot save your partner if you have hung a beacon around your neck and don't know how to use it to search. Proficiency with beacons requires diligent practice.

It is irresponsible to venture into the backcountry without a beacon. It might just save your life—not only if you are buried, but also if you back off when you are in a marginal situation instead of taking courage from your beacon. And even if you do not survive a burial, your body will be recovered relatively expediently, sparing your family and friends angst and limiting the exposure of rescuers to hazard during a prolonged search.

Probes are generally 8-10 feet (2.5-3 meters) long and are made in sections that quickly fit together. Some specially made ski poles also double as probes but most do not work as well as dedicated probes. Without a probe, it is impossible to thoroughly check out surface clues, to confirm the location of a completely buried person wearing a transmitting beacon (you will waste a lot of time digging if you are off by even a small distance), or to conduct a probe line for a completely buried person who is not wearing a beacon.

Shovels move snow roughly five times faster than your hands. The average depth of burial for avalanche victims in the U.S. is just over 3 feet or 1 meter. There are a number of good one and two-piece lightweight aluminum shovels with medium-size scoops. Some are made with snow saws inside the shafts. It may not matter if your partner is wearing a beacon if you don't have a shovel because you probably won't be able to dig quickly enough.

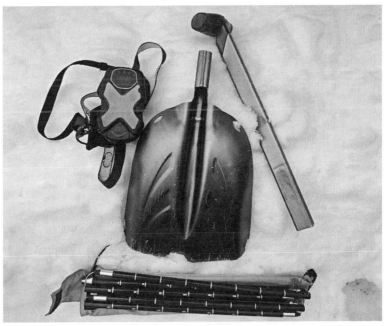

Basic avalanche rescue equipment for each person in the party includes a beacon, probe, shovel, and brain, all in operating order.

The Avalung™: This is a device that is designed to help you breathe oxygen from the snowpack and vent your deadly carbon dioxide exhalation away from the intake. The idea is that it can buy you a little time while your partners mount a search, assuming that you are able to get the mouthpiece into place when caught and that you are able to expand your chest when buried. Users also report that the Avalung is helpful during the avalanche, allowing them to breathe instead of having their mouths choked with snow. The Avalung must be worn outside your jacket or some models are integrated into a pack with the breathing tube in one of the pack straps. Thus far, Avalungs have been used mostly by skiers and snowboarders as it is difficult to fit the mouthpiece under a full face snowmobile helmet, but efforts are underway to correct this problem.

Avalanche Airbags: Developed in Europe, the survival statistics for victims wearing air bags are better than for any other rescue device available. Worn attached to a pack, a 40 gallon (150 liter) airbag inflates when you pull the ripcord. Since larger volume objects float to the surface, you are less likely to be completely or deeply buried, thus increasing your chance of survival. Even if you are buried, the brightly colored airbag may help others locate you quickly. Because airbags help victims ride higher in the debris, they may offer some protection from impact injuries, but death from trauma is still a major concern in any avalanche ride.

Here's a brief summary of the essentials of a backcountry rescue plan, both as a victim and as a rescuer.

RESCUE PLAN

As a Victim:

❉ If you are caught in an avalanche, call out so other members of your party know to watch you as you are carried down the slope, and then keep your mouth closed to prevent inhalation of snow. If you are wearing an Avalung, clamp down on the mouthpiece. You may have a split second to grab a tree, dig into the bed surface, or lunge, ski, snowboard, or throttle your machine off to the side. If so, do it! (Note: If you are inside a vehicle when caught, immediately shut off the engine to avoid the danger of carbon monoxide poisoning.)

114

✳ If possible, discard anything cumbersome such as skis, poles, snowshoes, or snowboard although this is much easier said than done. This gear tends to pull you underneath the surface of the moving snow. Unless your pack is extremely heavy, it is probably best to keep it on as it will help protect your spine, increase your volume (which may help keep you higher in the debris), and you may well need the emergency and first aid equipment contained within it.

✳ Use a swimming and rolling motion to try to stay on the surface of the snow and/or work your way out of the avalanche. FIGHT with all your effort. You will likely be out of control but try to keep your head upslope and your feet downslope and maneuver around fixed objects like trees and rocks. The main message is that now is the time to struggle to stay on the surface and to avoid hitting objects that could inflict mechanical injuries.

✳ As you feel the snow slow down, thrust your hand or any part of your body above the snow surface so that others can see it. You probably will be so disoriented that you won't know where the snow surface is so just guess and lunge.

✳ Before the snow comes to rest, cup your arm or hand in front of your face to clear an air space. If possible, try to expand your chest during this time.

✳ If buried, stop fighting and relax to preserve oxygen. Remember, you are not supposed to panic! Occasionally, buried victims have been found by yelling for help but usually the hearing of the rescuers is impaired by external noise (e.g., wind, rustling clothes, talking, the sound of footsteps, etc.). Victims can often hear more clearly because of the absence of this static under the snow. It is probably best to save your breath and yell only if you hear someone directly overhead.

As a Rescuer:

❋ Watch the victim as he/she is carried down the slope. If the victim disappears under the moving snow, keep your eyes fixed on the mass of snow he or she was enveloped in until it comes to rest. The victim may be under the snow surface in that area.

❋ Use the STOP and GO method. STOP means Stop, Think, Observe, Plan. GO means Go into action and Organize the rescuers. Take a deep breath. You are the victim's best chance of survival now. Stay on site and search. Almost all hope of a live rescue depends on you. Statistically, a victim has only a 50% chance of survival if buried about 25 minutes. The first 15 minutes are especially critical, with the greatest probability of a successful rescue. Outside help cannot usually arrive fast enough. You are dealing with a drowning person!

A Note Concerning Not Going for Help: A person buried under the snow needs air immediately, not hours later. If you have a group of four and you send one person for help, you are losing 25% of your search party. Think of how much searching each individual can do in a half hour or hour. One exception would be if help can be summoned without depriving the victim of your immediate aid (e.g., calling on a radio or cell phone) and another might be sending for assistance after hours of intense searching. Keep in mind that it often takes hours for help to arrive on scene. If you go for help, you are likely to end up with a body recovery, not a rescue.

❋ Before entering the search area, make sure there is no further avalanche danger along your approach route or at the site and pick a quick escape route understood by all. If the avalanche was human-triggered or occurred on a small slope, rescuers can probably go into the slide area safely, especially if they enter the path on snow that has already slid. If nearly the entire starting zone has released and no loading is taking place, it is highly unlikely that it will avalanche again. You do not have to be concerned about the fracture line releasing spontaneously (i.e., much weight has been removed from the slope and the trap has already been sprung). If it is storming or windy, observe the rate at which reloading is occurring. If a significant portion of the starting zone has not released and loading is still occurring, the possibility of a second avalanche may be high. The debris will not slide again but be careful of situations where multiple release zones funnel into a single runout zone or where other people approaching from above might trigger a release. Responding to an avalanche rescue can be extremely dangerous or fatal to rescuers who travel with disregard for existing avalanche hazard. Use the avalanche hazard evaluation checklist to evaluate the conditions and do not hesitate to halt the search if red lights are flashing. If significant hazard remains above the accident site or along the approach route, avalanche control (the artificial release of unstable snow using explosives) should be conducted before sending rescuers in to search.

❄ Take a few moments to organize the search party but then get moving—the clock is ticking. Delegate tasks, be systematic, and efficiently allocate your resources. Do not scatter gear belonging to the rescuers in the search area or it will soon be confused with possible clues. Keep the debris as free from contamination as possible (e.g., do not drop food, urinate, spit tobacco, spill fuel, or sit on the debris). If search dogs need to be called in, a clean site will enable them to perform better.

❄ Once at the site, mark the area where the victim was last seen and search downslope of this area. The last seen area, clues on the surface, and the avalanche fall-line may help establish the victim's downslope trajectory. How far a victim was carried depends on a number of factors (e.g., how long the person stayed on their feet or sled, the speed and magnitude of the avalanche, slope angle, path shape, and vertical drop). If you can limit the likely search area, you greatly increase the chances of a successful search.

✳ If you respond to an avalanche that has been witnessed by someone else, question the witness carefully about the number of victims, their last seen locations (or the relative location of each victim, including the witness, when the avalanche occurred), and whether the victims were wearing transmitting avalanche beacons. If at all possible, return to the accident site with the witness. If realistic and timely, place the witness in exactly the same spot he or she was standing when the avalanche occurred to make it easier to accurately pinpoint the last seen area of the victim(s). The witness is the best clue you have about what transpired, can help make sure you are searching in the right location, and can clear up critical questions as they arise on site.

Your *initial search* should consist of the following three tasks, preferably performed simultaneously. Avoid getting so focused on one task that you miss vital clues. We have, for example, repeatedly observed rescuers step right over an obvious clue (including a hand) while tracking a beacon signal. In another case, had the rescuer picked up a hat sitting on the snow surface, he would have seen the victim's head poking through the debris. You may laugh but this happens to all of us when under enormous pressure. Usually the best way to pull off the fastest possible rescue is to slow down just a little and be very deliberate.

✳ *Conduct a beacon search* of the entire deposition area unless it is positively known that the victim is not wearing a beacon. Make sure that *all* rescuers have switched their beacons to receive. If you are wearing a beacon, you should have already practiced with it many times because your partner's life depends upon your proficiency. After pinpointing the signal, probe to confirm the victim's exact location before digging.

❄ *Thoroughly search for clues* such as a snowmobile ski sticking out of the snow or a hat on the debris. Clues may be very subtle. They might include entry or exit tracks, drops

These are obvious clues. Be sure to probe under and around them. Don't forget to pull on the ski pole. Mark or leave all clues in place.

of blood, a piece of hair, a snowshoe strap, a suspiciously dark area between snow blocks, a muffled scratching sound, or the family dog sitting in one location. Check out all clues by pulling on them and/or probing underneath and around them. Leave the clues in place (mark them if they are hard to see) and alert the other members of your party of their existence. Move fast but take the time to look and listen carefully and be sure to cover the entire search area.

❄ *Spot probe likely areas* including obstacles (e.g., trees or rocks) or areas where the debris is apt to pile up such as benches, dips, and bends. Make sure to probe under and around clues. Spot probing, also known as random probing, means searching for a buried victim by pushing an avalanche probe vertically into the snow. The procedure is random in the sense that no particular grid pattern is used but you need to systematically search likely spots. The golden rule of probing is "probe unto others as you would have them probe unto you." In other words, do not jam the probe into the snow but use it as a sounding rod to feel what lies below. The danger of hurting someone with a probe is less than the danger of the victim running out of air. If you wonder what it will feel like to probe a body, take a probe and poke yourself or, better yet, a friend. Springy branches and unfrozen ground can feel like a body. The deeper the burial, the greater your uncertainty is likely to be. When it doubt about a possible strike, check it out! Always keep your shovel with you so that you don't lose precious seconds.

The first responders to an avalanche accident have spread out across the debris and are systematically searching the entire deposition zone. Their initial search consists of conducting a beacon search, looking and listening for clues, and spot probing likely catchment areas.

❋ If the victim is not located after a very thorough initial search of the entire search or deposition area, begin a *coarse probe* in the most likely catchment area. (Note: If you only have one or two searchers, it may be best to continue spot probing likely areas unless the prime search area is very small. The same is true if you are very unsure of the most likely search area.) Spread out, in a horizontal line, with your arms outstretched to the side and touching the fingertips of the person next to you. If you are tall, draw your arms in slightly. Holding the probes vertically, each prober will probe left, center, and right before advancing as a line. You are trying to achieve a distance of 20 inches (50 centimeters) between probe holes. This grid spacing, which represents a compromise between thoroughness and the speed necessary to maximize the chances of recovering a buried victim alive, yields roughly an 88% probability that the victim will be found on the first pass. The probability of encounter increases slightly with each pass. It is important that the grid spacing be maintained; otherwise, you are just taking a lot of time to do a "random probe." The verbal commands, preferably spoken by one person at the end of the line are "probe left, probe center, probe right, advance." A 20 inch (50 centimeter) advance is slightly less than an arm's length. Move the probe first, then step up to it. Always advance on the side where you have just finished probing as it is easier to judge distance straight ahead than on a diagonal. It is best to move the line uphill rather than downhill as this will facilitate keeping the spacing together and is a bit gentler on the backs of the rescuers. Keep the line moving!

Coarse probe lines are used to search for victims who are completely buried without transmitting beacons. To improve your chances of success with this primitive search method, identify the most likely search areas, advance uphill, keep the grid spacing consistent, and move efficiently. (Photo by Bill Glude)

All probe lines should work fast, efficiently, and quietly. If you are sure that you are probing the right area, then after you have completed a pass, offset your line (to the left or right, whichever direction makes more sense) and probe the area again. If you think, but are not absolutely sure that you have probed the buried person, leave your probe in place, have a second person quickly check it out, note the depth, and start digging. If you are uncertain, always investigate by digging. When you drop out of the line, the rest of the probe team should close in the spacing and keep advancing until your find is confirmed. Otherwise, a great deal of time can be lost while digging out false strikes. If you do not find the victim in the primary search area after multiple passes, at some point you may need to expand the search area to include the next most likely area and repeat the steps above.

❋   When you locate a victim, dig fast but carefully (see note below about shoveling strategy), taking care not to trample the victim's air space. If possible, excavate the person's head and chest first. Rather than "yanking" the victim from the debris, first conduct a careful primary and secondary survey. Treatment for suffocation, hypothermia, mechanical injuries, and/ or shock is commonly required.

A Note about Shoveling Strategy: Shoveling can be the most time-consuming and tiring part of any rescue. If you can move the least amount of snow possible, as fast as possible, you will increase the victim's chance of survival. It is easy for rescuers to inadvertently end up with a funnel-shaped hole, with the victim wedged in the bottom and snow cascading back over the lip. Initially, leave the probe that has struck the buried person in place, and move downhill a distance equal to 1.5 times the burial depth. In other words, if the probe indicates that the person is buried 3 feet (1 meter) deep, move 4.5 feet (1.5 meters) downhill. If you have only one or two rescuers, kneel and start moving the debris off to the side (not downhill) with a canoe stroke. You will be much more efficient if you keep the shovel below your waist rather than trying to lift the snow. Once you have excavated a thigh deep hole, stand inside and throw the debris downhill. The objective is to move snow only once. If more rescuers are available, fan downhill in an inverted V with the primary shoveler at the apex and all others moving snow like a conveyor belt out of the way. Rotate the head digger frequently as this is the most arduous position. By creating a ramp leading to the victim, this technique is the fastest means of extrication. Another advantage of this method is that rescuers are less likely to be standing on the victim and trampling critical air space. Be aware that patients will cool rapidly as they are excavated from the snow.

Note that these shovelers have begun digging downslope of the probe strike and are coordinating their efforts. This will significantly reduce the amount of time needed to uncover the victim. (Photo by Dale Atkins)

❄ ❄ ❄ ❄

How long do you search? Continue searching until you find the victim, all hope is lost, or until the hazard to rescuers is too great due to exhaustion, hypothermia, increasing avalanche hazard, or other complications. Darkness alone is not a reason to call off a search. Give the victim the benefit of the doubt. Some victims have been dug out dead after only a few minutes but under exceptional conditions, some have lived for hours and even longer.

Common mistakes in avalanche rescues include: poor organization (e.g., no rescue plan, uncertain leadership, lack of rescue gear) and conducting an inadequate initial search (e.g., not doing one, not searching the entire area, not knowing how to use a beacon, not turning all beacons worn by witnesses, survivors, and searchers to receive, not locating surface clues or spot probing likely areas). An initial search is also known as a hasty search. We discourage use of the latter term because it seems to promote the above errors, which often result in a body recovery rather than a successful rescue. An initial search must be both thorough *and* fast.

Being able to respond effectively in a crisis situation requires preparation. Have a rescue plan. The first time you and your partners discuss rescue should not be after an accident has just occurred. Practice beacon searches regularly. Once a week, all winter long is not too often; twice a year is too little. Organize and run probe lines. Set up simulated rescue scenarios to which you or your partners respond. Spring some of these as surprises. Whenever possible, practice all the elements of rescue on avalanche debris.

SUMMARY OF THE NECESSARY COMPONENTS
OF A SUCCESSFUL RESCUE

- Having a plan (knowing how and where to search)
- *Speed* tempered with *safety*
- Leadership
- Communication
- Efficient allocation of resources
- Qualified searchers
- Necessary equipment
- First aid/evacuation
- Self-help!

Looking Ahead

You have several choices in your approach to winter travel in the mountains. You can hone your traveling abilities, without working much on your avalanche hazard evaluation skills. By doing so, you are essentially playing Russian roulette with Nature. Most of the time you spin the chamber you will win, but the consequences of losing will likely be unacceptable. Or, conversely, you can become completely paranoid about every snow-covered slope and never be able to travel anywhere because you always have your head in a snowpit. Best yet, you can arm yourself with knowledge. The way we see it, learning how to evaluate avalanche hazard is an investment in your future.

This book is a start. Re-read it at least a few times. Make sure your partners do the same. You can build on your avalanche hazard evaluation skills in a variety of ways. When you are traveling, tune in all of your senses. If you vow to pay attention and heed the message, you never need get caught in an avalanche. Participate in a top quality avalanche workshop, taught by avalanche professionals, with field-oriented training. Read more books, watch avalanche videos, do online tutorials. Seek partners with good avalanche skills and listen, learn, and question. Track the avalanche forecasts in your area throughout the season, even on days you are not heading into the mountains, so that you are better able to anticipate and understand the changes in snow stability. Measure slope angles frequently with your inclinometer and record the angles of your favorite slopes. Study the snowpack in a given area to see how the layers change over time. Keep a notebook in which you record weather and snowpack observations, related avalanche events, and comments. Teach others what you know and, in the process, you will learn more—both about avalanches and communication. Study avalanches that have released, trying to piece together the contributory factors. Learn from 20/20 hindsight by scrutinizing avalanche accidents. Even from media reports, if you look deeper than the sound bites inevitably expressing surprise because the victims were so "experienced," you can usually identify the red light factors. Keep learning and don't let yourself be dissuaded from the facts. To paraphrase Andre Roch, a venerable Swiss pioneer of avalanche science, "Remember, the avalanche does not know you are an expert." Our bet is that the return on your investment is that you will enjoy the mountains more than ever. Good luck and have fun.

We wish you many happy, safe, and spectacular days in the mountains.

Additional Information

RESOURCES FOR FURTHER LEARNING

The lists below are not comprehensive, but they are a start.

Avalanche Safety Texts:

Jamieson, B., D. Svederus, and L. Zacaruk. 2007. *Sledding in Avalanche Terrain: Reducing the Risk*, Canadian Avalanche Association, Revelstoke, British Columbia, 74 pages.

McClung, D.M. and P.A. Schaerer. 2006, *The Avalanche Handbook*, The Mountaineers Books, Seattle, Washington, 342 pages.

Tremper, B. 2008. *Staying Alive in Avalanche Terrain.* The Mountaineers Books, Seattle, Washington, 318 pages.

General Reading/Learning from 20/20 Hindsight:

Fredston, J.A., 2005, *Snowstruck: In the Grip of Avalanches*, Harcourt, Inc., New York, New York, 342 pages.

Jamieson, B., P. Haegli, and D. Gauthier. 2010. *Avalanche Accidents in Canada: Volume 5, 1996-2007*, Canadian Avalanche Association, Revelstoke, British Columbia, 432 pages.

Also: *The Avalanche Review*. Periodical published 4 times yearly. For subscription information contact: American Association of Avalanche Professionals, P.O. Box 247, Pagosa Springs, Colorado, 81147.

Web Tutorials/Videos:

http://avalanche.org/tutorial/tutorial.html
(American Avalanche Association)

http://www.avalanche.ca/cac/training/online-course
(Canadian Avalanche Association)

http://www.fsavalanche.com
(U.S. Forest Service National Avalanche Center)

www.tetongravity.com/snowlab/avi_education_videos.aspx
 (Teton Gravity Research avalanche education videos)

The Fine Line (avalanche video by Rocky Mountain Sherpas,
available http://sherpascinema.com/store)

SELECTED INTERNET ADDRESSES

These sites link to avalanche advisories, accident reports, avalanche
schools, and more.

http://www.avalanche.org (United States)

http://www.avalanche.ca (Canada)

http://www.avalanches.org (European Avalanche Warning Services)

http:www.lawinenwarndienst.ktn.gv.at (Austria)

http://www.france.meteofrance.com (France)

http://en.vedur.is/avalanches/articles (Iceland)

http://www.avalanche.net.nz (New Zealand)

http:www.ngi.no/snoskred (Norway)

http://www.slf.ch (Switzerland)

NORTH AMERICAN PUBLIC AVALANCHE DANGER SCALE

Avalanche danger is determined by the likelihood, size and distribution of avalanches.

Danger Level	Travel Advice	Likelihood of Avalanches	Avalanche Size and Distribution
5 Extreme	Avoid all avalanche terrain.	Natural and human-triggered avalanches certain.	Large to very large avalanches in many areas.
4 High	Very dangerous avalanche conditions. Travel in avalanche terrain not recommended.	Natural avalanches likely; human-triggered avalanches very likely.	Large avalanches in many areas; or very large avalanches in specific areas.
3 Considerable	Dangerous avalanche conditions. Careful snowpack evaluation, cautious route-finding and conservative decision-making essential.	Natural avalanches possible; human-triggered avalanches likely.	Small avalanches in many areas; or large avalanches in specific areas; or very large avalanches in isolated areas.
2 Moderate	Heightened avalanche conditions on specific terrain features. Evaluate snow and terrain carefully; identify features of concern.	Natural avalanches unlikely; human-triggered avalanches possible.	Heightened avalanche conditions on specific terrain features. Evaluate snow and terrain carefully; identify features of concern.
1 Low	Generally safe avalanche conditions. Watch for unstable snow on isolated terrain features.	Natural and human-triggered avalanches unlikely.	Small avalanches in isolated areas or extreme terrain.

Safe backcountry travel requires training and experience. You control your own risk by choosing where, when and how you travel.

Scale adopted 2010

Acknowledgments

Avalanches introduced us to one another, taught us to pay attention, to look forward and back, and to keep evaluating. In showing us death, avalanches have strongly influenced how we have chosen to live our lives. If you spend time with those who live and breathe avalanches, you will notice that they speak a strange but universal language. Those fluent in snow can go anywhere in the world and read the history of the winter's weather as inscribed in the layers of the snowpack. You will likely also observe that the community of avalanche workers is as unique as snow itself. It is comprised of individuals from a huge diversity of backgrounds and countries, fired by perpetual curiosity and united by a common passion.

Nurtured by this community since we first began trying to understand the union of circumstances that make avalanches and avalanche accidents possible, we can never come close to thanking all those who have added dimension to our perspective. Nearly thirty years have unfolded since the first edition of *Snow Sense* and many generations of ideas are embedded in these pages. The four of us remember, with gratitude, some of our earliest mentors including Ed LaChapelle, John Montagne, Kent Saxton, and Norm Wilson. We have benefited greatly from the work and support of Dale Atkins, Don Bachman, Jim Bay, Bob Brown, Paul Burke, Bruce Edgerly, Roland Emetaz, Dale Gallagher, Manuel Genswein, Bill Glude, Ethan Greene, Garrett Grove, Joachim Heierli, Dave Hendrickson, Bruce Jamieson, Art Judson, Janet Kellam, Pete Martinelli, Art Mears, Ian Mc-Cammon, Dave McClung, Kip Melling, Rod Newcomb, Chuck O'Leary, Nick Parker, Marcus Peterson, Ron Perla, Nancy Pfeiffer, Peter Schaerer, Ron Simenhois, Blaine Smith, Juerg Sweitzer, Bruce Tremper, Alec van Herwijnen, Knox Williams, Paul Wunnicke and many, many others.

Doug and Jill owe tremendous thanks to our editors for their enthusiastic and unflagging help on this edition despite the logistical difficulties of being separated by a hemisphere and an expanse of ocean. Karl and Doug are more than dedicated, insightful, outstanding avalanche profession-als—they are graceful human beings whom we are proud to claim as friends. And finally, the two of us bow our heads to Arthur and Elinor Fredston for years of unstinting encouragement.

ABOUT THE AUTHORS:

Jill Fredston and Doug Fesler have spent more than three decades evaluating avalanche hazard, predicting avalanches, triggering them with explosives, teaching potential victims how to stay alive, and leading rescue efforts in Alaska.

Doug Fesler

Doug's interest in avalanches intensified in the early 1970s when, as a park ranger, he began to recover the bodies of avalanche victims from places he wouldn't have thought twice about going himself. An innovator in avalanche education, he was instrumental in drawing attention to the role of "human factors" in causing avalanche accidents. He is the founder of the acclaimed Alaska Avalanche School, former chief of the State of Alaska Snow Avalanche Safety Program, and was an active member of the Alaska Mountain Rescue Group for 30 years.

(Photo by Anne Raup)
Jill Fredston

Jill's childhood fascination with snow led her to a master's degree in polar studies/snow and ice and extensive field work in Alaska, northern Canada, and Greenland. She is the former director of the Alaska Avalanche Forecast Center and the Alaska Avalanche School and has served as accident site commander on dozens of avalanche search missions. Jill is the author of *Snowstruck: In the Grip of Avalanches* and *Rowing to Latitude: Journeys Along the Arctic's Edge*, which won the 2002 National Outdoor Book Award. She speaks professionally about decision-making and strategies for dealing with risk, uncertainty, and change.

Since 1986, Jill and Doug have co-directed the Alaska Mountain Safety Center, Inc., a non-profit organization they founded to promote public safety primarily through avalanche education and hazard management consulting. Taking summers off, they have rowed more than 25,000 miles along the coasts of Alaska, Canada, Greenland, Spitsbergen, and

Norway in two small boats. More recently, they have set sail along the Pacific coast from Alaska to the tip of South America.

ABOUT THE EDITORS:

(Photo by Jennifer Chipman)

Karl Birkeland

Karl Birkeland is the Avalanche Scientist for the U.S. Forest Service National Avalanche Center. In addition to conducting extensive avalanche research, he works to transfer emerging science and technologies to field practitioners within the avalanche community. Karl is also an adjunct Professor of Earth Sciences at Montana State University where he supervises a number of graduate students. Karl's professional work with avalanches as a ski patroller, educator, backcountry forecaster, and researcher spans over 30 years. He founded the Gallatin National Forest Avalanche Center (Montana) and earned both his MS and PhD degrees investigating snowpack variability and related ramifications for avalanche forecasting. When he is not working in the snow, Karl enjoys spending as much time as possible in the mountains and on rivers with his wife and two daughters.

Doug Chabot

Doug Chabot has been the director of the Gallatin National Forest Avalanche Center (Montana) since 2000. From 1990 to 1998 he was a professional ski patroller at nearby Bridger Bowl Ski Area. Doug is a leader in snowmobile avalanche education and founder of SnowPilot, a free snowpit graphing and database software program for snow professionals. Doug has worked as a mountain guide since 1989, participated in sixteen Alaskan climbing expeditions, and undertaken major climbs in Nepal, India, Afghanistan and Pakistan, some of which have been first ascents. Since 2005, Doug has spent summers doing educational and humanitarian work in Afghanistan and Pakistan. In 2011, Doug and his wife, Genevieve, co-founded Iqra Fund (www.iqrafund.org) to help provide education for girls in Pakistan and Morocco.